Multidisciplinary Perspectives on Language Competence

Edited by Rita Cancino & Lotte Dam

AALBORG UNIVERSITY PRESS

Multidisciplinary Perspectives on Language Competence
Edited by Rita Cancino & Lotte Dam

1st Edition

© The editors and Aalborg University Press, 2014

Layout: Hofdamerne ApS v/ Cecilie von Haffner & Lea Rathnov
Printed in Denmark by Toptryk Grafisk ApS, 2014

ISBN: 978-87-7112-187-2

Published by:
Aalborg University Press
Skjernvej 4A, 2nd floor
DK – 9220 Aalborg Ø
Phone: +45 99407140
aauf@forlag.aau.dk
forlag.aau.dk

This book is published with financial support from Lillian og Dan Finks Fond, Videnskabernes Selskab and the Department of Culture and Global Studies, Aalborg University.

All rights reserved. No part of this book may be reprinted or reproduced or utilized in any form or by any electronic, mechanical, or other means, now known or hereafter invented, including photocopying and recording, or in any information storage or retrieval system, without permission in writing from the publishers, except for reviews and short excerpts in scholarly publications.

Preface	5
Towards a multidisciplinary perspective on language competence *Rita Cancino & Lotte Dam*	7
Correlation between theoretical knowledge of grammar and performance in the production of written texts *Richard Madsen*	23
Effects of forward lexical transfer on formality level as an L2 English competency *Jesper Bonderup Frederiksen*	61
LSP and sociocultural competences. The teaching of comparative Spanish legal language at a Danish university *Rita Cancino*	87
Text competence – a challenge in German legal contracts *Aase Voldgaard Larsen*	111
Instructional Semantics and linguistic competence *Lotte Dam*	135
Performance and competence in usage-based construction grammar *Kim Ebensgaard Jensen*	157
Linguistic Competences: Do they really need improving? *Anna Kristina Hultgren*	189
Contributors	214

Preface

The papers in this book are written by a group of scholars whose research treat different aspects of English, German, or Spanish. As researchers and teachers in foreign languages we are interested in different dimensions of language competences, and our aim is to provide new angles on these competences in areas such as business communications, legal language, grammar, and within the service sector.

Multidisciplinary Perspectives on Language Competence thus intends to provide a different and broader view on the importance of language and foreign language competences and the various faces these concepts show in our multicultural and multilingual societies. It is our hope that this book may answer some of the often raised questions on language competence in both practical and principled ways. The target audience of this book is students and teachers in higher education institutions and employees of international companies.

Finally, we want to thank Lillian og Dan Finks Fond, Videnskabernes Selskab, and the Department of Culture and Global Studies, Aalborg University, for the funding and financial support we received for this publication.

Rita Cancino and Lotte Dam, Aalborg June 2014

Towards a multidisciplinary perspective on language competence

The concept of *language competence* appears in a variety of contexts and is applied in connection with both native languages (for example, it may cover both young children's native language skills and adults' ability to use their language in particular professional contexts) and to second languages (such as the language skills of immigrant children and foreign language students). Unsurprisingly, *competence* is not an unambiguous concept and has been a subject of much discussion in the fields of general and applied linguistics (see Bagarić and Djigunovi 2007, 94). The concept *linguistic competence* was introduced by Chomsky (1965, 4) in his sharp distinction between *linguistic competence* (people's (tacit) knowledge of language) and *linguistic performance* (language usage). This distinction has served as point of departure of later approaches. Many of these are even critical toward Chomsky's distinction and use it to position their own concepts of language competence (e.g. Hymes, 1972 and Paradis, 2003). For example, functionalist approaches (such as cognitive linguistics and sociolinguistics) are known to be critical toward Chomsky's division and tend to dismiss the sharp distinction between competence and performance. Soon after Chomsky's proposal, advocates of a communicative perspective in applied linguistics expressed a strong disapproval of the idea of using the concept of idealized, purely linguistic competence as a theoretical foundation of learning, teaching and testing language skills (Bagarić and Djigunović, 2007, 95). Instead, the concept *communicative competence*, proposed by Dell Hymes, has gained ground (Hymes, 1972). This concept focuses on socially situated performance, and as such brings a sociolinguistic perspective to bear on *competence*. Since its introduction, the concept of communicative competence has seen further development in various directions within applied linguistics, and new terms have been proposed, such as *language proficiency* and *communicative language ability*. Such terms are conceptually close to the notion of communicative competence: they all refer to knowledge of and skills in language use (Bagarić and Djigunović 2007, 100).

Bagarić and Djigunović (2007) provide an overview of different, but related, models of communicative competence. In the following, we will discuss three notions that recur across these models; for a full exposition of the models, see Bagarić and Djigunović (2007). According to Bagarić and Djigunović (2007, 97), recent theoretical and empirical research on communicative competence is largely based on models proposed by Michael Canale and Merril Swain (see Canale and Swain, 1980, 1981; Canale, 1983, 1984) and Lyle Bachman and Adrian Palmer (see Bachman, 1990; Bachman and Palmer, 1996) as well as the description of components of communicative language competence in the Common European Framework (CEF). Three types of competences recur in the models: *linguistic competence*, *sociolinguistic competence*, and *discursive/textual competence*. Generally speaking, *linguistic competence* refers to the mastery of the linguistic code – morphology, syntax, vocabulary, etc. – that enables the speaker to use the knowledge and skills needed for understanding and expressing meanings. *Sociolinguistic competence* refers to the mastery of the sociocultural code of language use – namely, rules and conventions for appropriate comprehension and language use in a particular social context. *Discursive/textual competence* refers to the mastery of combining language structures into meaningful texts and text types. Content-wise the models are very similar, but the criteria for distinguishing between different types of competence are not exactly the same. For example, an element which in one model belongs to linguistic competence, belongs to discourse competence in another model. In the following we will elaborate on the three different types of competence.

Linguistic competence
Linguistic code refers to the language system itself and embraces the symbolic nature of linguistic items: they combine form with conventional meaning. According to Tomasello (2003, 8), linguistic symbols are social conventions through which one individual attempts to share attention with another individual by directing the other individual's attentional or mental state to something in the outside world. At a general level, mastering the linguistic code means that the language user is able to express and understand meaningful language. In a communication situation, the speaker uses the language code to construct linguistic meaning, and the addressee uses the language code to decode this meaning. The nature of linguistic conventions differs in the various areas of language competence. Whereas, say, orthography and phonetics primarily concern conventionalized rules (spelling and pronunciation) of language structure, the conventions of use of lexical items and functional items also concern semantics. It is, however, possible to communicate meanings without mastering the linguistic code in its entirety. For example, it is possible to understand spoken and written texts with grammatical and orthographical errors and to understand young children's utterance even if they only use nouns. However, it goes without saying that it requires a high level of linguistic competence to communicate and understand more complex meanings and to use the proper register according to the context in question. Mastering the linguistic code does not necessarily equal having declarative knowledge about linguistic items. For instance, most native speakers of a given language, including children, are likely to know how and when to use, say, definite descriptions and inversion without knowing why.

Linguistic competence is an object of study in more theoretically oriented frameworks within general linguistics as well as in applied linguistics. Researchers with different interests address linguistic competence, such as researchers with an interest in how linguistic meaning is constructed in the mind of language users, and functionalist linguists with an interest in describing the functionality of specific linguistic constructions. Such areas strive to account for the way in which linguistic items contribute to meaning creation and as such form part of language users' linguistic competence at a more general level (with a focus on language description, and with less focus on language competence at an individual level).

Tomasello (2003), which represents a usage-based approach to language acquisition, is an important contribution to the study of language competence. The usage-based view on language is shared by cognitive-functional linguists, such as Langacker (1987, 1992), Goldberg (2006), and Bybee (2010). Their central processing tenet is that language structure emerges from language use (Tomasello 2003, 5). In the usage-based approach, natural language competence consists not only of highly abstract syntactic constructions, but also concrete expressions based on individual words or phrases, such as ritualized greetings, idioms, metaphors, and noncanonical phrasal collocations (Tomasello 2003, 5-6). This view on language competence is consistent with a more communicative view on competence.

It goes without saying that the areas of first and second language acquisition (including studies in bilingualism) are concerned directly with how humans achieve linguistic competence. Due to the immense number of contributions within these fields, it is not possible to present a detailed outline of how linguistic competence figures in these areas; interested readers are referred to Bruner (1985), Tomasello (2003), Ellis (1997; 2008) and Gass and Selinker (2008).

Sociolinguistic and sociocultural competence
Research articles about language, language learning, culture and foreign languages use many different terms and concepts when describing the competences which are necessary to acquire in order to communicate appropriately in the context of a given culture. *Sociolinguistic or sociocultural competences* are particularly important in foreign language learning.

Before treating the concepts of *sociolinguistic and sociocultural competence*, we will provide a few brief definitions of the most frequently used terms within second language acquisition in an attempt to clarify the confusing world of concepts used about cultural competences.

In the educational sector, *cultural competence* has been defined as "the ability to successfully teach students who come from different cultures other than your own" (Diller & Moule, 2005, 2). According to Cross (in Diller and Moule: 2005, 12), "*cultural competence* is a set of congruent behaviors, attitudes, and policies that come together in a system, agency, or among professionals and enable that system, agency, or those professionals to work effectively in cross-cultural situations". Hence, the ability to be culturally competent is central in increasing understanding and improving relationships across cultures.

Several definitions of *intercultural competence* figure in the literature. According to Barret et al. (2013, 7),

> 'intercultural competence' is a combination of attitudes, knowledge, understanding and skills applied through action, which enables one, either singly or together with others, to understand and respect people who are perceived to have different cultural affiliations from oneself; to respond appropriately, effectively and respectfully when interacting and communicating with such people; to establish positive and constructive relationships with such people and to understand oneself and one's own multiple cultural affiliations through encounters with cultural 'difference'.

Trans-cultural competence has been defined by Seidl (1998, 107) as the competence "which combines both knowledge about culture and the ability to apply this knowledge appropriately".

The terms *sociolinguistic competence* and *sociolinguistic knowledge* are mostly used in the sense of *sociocultural competence*. Byram (2010) also includes the concept of *social competence* as it is closely connected to this competence. *Sociocultural competence* refers to a speaker's familiarity with the social processes and practices related to any specific language use situation. *Social competence* refers to "the will and the skill to interact with others" (Byram 1997, 10). In a discussion of *intercultural competence*, Kramsch (2010; also Kramsch and Whiteside, 2008) appears to emphasise the value of Byram's notion of *social competence*. He argues that the development of such competence is not only a question of tolerance towards or empathy with others, of understanding them in their cultural context, or of understanding oneself and the other in terms of one another, but also a matter of looking beyond words and actions and embracing multiple, changing and conflicting discourse worlds, in which

> [...] the circulation of values and identities across cultures, the inversions, even inventions of meaning, [are] often hidden behind a common illusion of effective communication ... while communicative competence was based on an assumption of understanding based on common goals and common interests, intercultural competence presupposes a lack of understanding due to divergent subjectivities and historicities.
> (Kramsch 2010, 3).

According to CEF (2005), *sociocultural competence* involves five elements: *Attitudes:* curiosity and openness, readiness to suspend disbelief about other cultures and belief about one's own. *Knowledge:* of social groups and their products and practices. *Skills of interpreting and relating:* ability to interpret a document or event from another culture. *Skills of discovery and interaction:* ability to acquire new knowledge of a culture and cultural practices and *Critical cultural awareness/political education:* ability to evaluate critically and on the basis of explicit criteria perspectives, practices and products in one's own and other cultures and countries.

In this context, the most important skills are the skills of interpreting and relating, which are the ability to interpret a document or event from another culture, to explain it and to relate it to documents from one's own culture. According to Byram, Gribkova and Starkey (2002, 8) skills are just as important as attitudes and knowledge.

> By putting ideas, events, documents from two or more cultures side by side and seeing how each might look from the other perspective, intercultural speakers/mediators can see how people might misunderstand what is said or written or done by somebody with a different social identity. The skills of comparison, of interpreting and relating, are therefore crucial.

Social identities are related to culture, and a person brought up in a specific community unconsciously learns the beliefs, values and behavior of this specific community. An intercultural speaker needs some awareness and knowledge, about what it means to be understood from the other persons' perspective. Consequently, skills, attitudes and values are involved, and learners need to acquire interest in and curiosity about 'otherness' and an awareness of themselves and their own cultures seen from other perspectives (Byram, Gribkova and Starkey, 2002)

Discursive and textual competence/knowledge
Discursive competence is used with reference to two related, but distinct, abilities. Researchers point out that there are different varieties of discursive competence that measure different aspects of communication. A very common type of competence related to discourse is 'rhetorical' or 'effective discourse competence'. This is often defined as referring to how well an individual can contribute to a conversation. This kind of discourse competence includes multiple components. One such component is how well the individual can understand what is being said by a range of speakers. Another component is how well the individual can interject his or her own opinions and how well that person can express ideas to an audience within a general scenario (Belmonte & McCabe, 2004). CEF (2001) defines *discourse competence* as "the ability of a user/learner to arrange sentences in sequence so as to produce coherent stretches of language".

A specific kind of competence in discourse, which is often called *textual discourse competence* or only *textual competence*, has been described by Ressurrecció et al., (2008) as a part of the translation process: "The *textual competence* consists in being proficient in combining linguistic forms to produce a written or oral text in different genres or text types". Here this type of competence covers the ability to understand and construct written texts of different genres, such as literary narratives, instructional guides, technical materials, procedural texts, expository texts, persuasive texts, descriptions and other types of written communications, like transcriptions of recorded conversations. Such discourse genres have different characteristics, but in each genre there are some elements that help make the text coherent, and other elements which are used to make important points distinctive or prominent. This competence is basically a measure of how well an individual can read different texts and understand them. The better readers can understand these texts, the more textual discourse competence they have.

Contributions

The present publication contains contributions about language in general, native languages and foreign languages. It follows a communicative approach to language, although we use the term *language competence* in the title instead of *communicative competence* (or others of its variants). We do this to emphasize that we focus on *language (communication* is broader) – although always in relation to real situations.

In *Correlation between theoretical knowledge of grammar and performance*, Richard Madsen provides a pilot study, which is part of a larger project whose goal is to investigate Danish university students' acquisition of English. The paper is a case study of the performance of a group of freshmen in the subjects of English Grammar and Production of Written Genres. Madsen quantifies, analyses and compares the students' results in an exam in theoretical grammar and their written home assignments. The analysis has three purposes. The primary one is to gain in-depth knowledge of status quo, i.e. how far the students have advanced in their acquisition of English and which areas of English pose the greatest difficulties to them. The secondary purpose is to see whether there is a correlation between knowledge of theoretical grammar and actual performance in the production of written texts – that is, a correlation between knowing grammar and being able to use it. By comparing how well the students do in theoretical grammar and how well they write English, it will be possible to provide some preliminary insights into the usefulness of teaching theoretical grammar with the purpose of facilitating the acquisition of a second language. The tertiary purpose of the analysis is to come up with some preliminary suggestions as to fine-tuning the above-mentioned courses in order better to promote the students' acquisition of English.

Effects of forward lexical transfer on formality level as an L2 English competency by Jesper Bonderup Frederiksen falls within the scope of crosslinguistic influence. According to this paper, the effects of lexical crosslinguistic influence on formality have been a neglected area, and Frederiksen suggests that the case of L2 English seems particularly worthy of attention due to the special character of the English lexicon as a mixture of vocabulary of mainly Germanic and Latinate origin. By way of example, most English words that are cognates for Danish students are of Germanic origin, whereas most words that are cognates for Spanish students are of Latinate origin. The paper focuses on the possible effects of forward lexical transfer on the level of formality as a language competence in L2 English and aims to test the specific hypothesis that Danish university students of English whose L1 is Danish use lexis of Germanic origin to a larger extent in L2 English than do Spanish university students of English whose L1 is Spanish. The hypothesis is being tested through an experiment currently in progress, and preliminary results indicate that Danish L2 English users choose a high proportion of Germanic words.

In *LSP and sociocultural competences: The teaching of comparative Spanish legal language at a Danish university*, Rita Cancino questions the possibility of separating culture from language, not only from language in general, but also from specialized language. Traditionally, foreign languages are taught as if language and culture were two ontologically distinct phenomena. In particular, culture as a concept is typically not associated with legal language, even if it is probably the most culture-bound professional language. The paper discusses whether it is possible to teach comparative legal Danish and legal Spanish without also teaching culture, as culture is embedded in legal terms that reflect the respective countries' histories, cultures and societal developments. Because of this, a legal term in one language is often without an equivalent in the other language. This represents a major challenge to the Danish students in their comparative studies of Danish and Spanish legal languages as they have poor knowledge of the Danish legal system and no knowledge of the Spanish legal system. The paper gives a short description of the complexity of legal language and, by means of examples from Danish and Spanish legal languages, some fundamental problems of 'translating' culture-bound legal terms from one legal-linguaculture into another are discussed.

The main purpose of *Text competence – a challenge in German legal contracts* by Aase Voldgaard Larsen explores the types of text competence required to be exercised in German tenancy contracts in order to ensure that the parties to a contract understand the text. Voldgaard also addresses the strategies used in the production process to meet lacking text competences. Text competence must be present with the parties, and text producers must be aware of the challenge they face when producing a contract text. A special type of problem occurs when one of the parties is a layperson who has no special insight into the subject of the contract, into the language of contracts and into the situation and function of the contract text. The paper draws on two surveys among German lawyers which show that, when formulating contract texts, text producers decide between emphasising a particular party perspective and thus the action-directing function or focusing on the court perspective and the control-directing function. Depending on which strategy they choose, their focus is to some extent on the contract comprehensibility for the layperson. On the basis of two German surveys, Larsen investigates the linguistic strategies that are utilized by text producers to meet the lacking text competences of the layperson. Finally, she examines if the strategies mentioned by the lawyers can be found in the wording of a 'layperson-friendly' contract.

The main purpose of *Instructional Semantics and linguistic competence* by Lotte Dam is to provide a detailed account of how linguistic meaning is produced and understood by speakers and addressees. Focusing on language itself, which, with its inherent properties, is used to create meaningful utterances in communication, the paper suggests that the theory of Instructional Semantics (IS) provides an operative framework for explaining the establishment of linguistic meaning. IS rests on the assumption that an utterance consists of three phases: input, process and product. The input for the process is language, which is used to create an utterance in a certain context. Once an utterance has been produced, an interpretive process is initiated in the addressee's mind. The product of this interpretive process is the establishment of meaning. In this process, the linguistic input is thought of as *instructions* for the addressee to perform an act of interpretation. By using the well-known distinction between lexical and functional items, the paper explains in more detail the properties of the instructions and how they interact in the establishment of meaning. After this account, the paper suggests to incorporate IS in second language teaching. It is argued that the principles of IS can contribute to the improvement of linguistic competence in a foreign language grammar and that grammar classes can benefit from them. This part of the paper also provides ideas for the make-up of grammar classes.

In *Performance and competence in usage-based construction grammar*, Kim Ebensgaard Jensen explores the interplay between performance and competence in the [V *until* ADJ]-construction in a construction grammar perspective. In usage-based models of language, performance and competence are considered to be in a mutually influential relation. The paper is based on the idea that language competence is influenced by language performance to the extent that linguistic phenomena cannot be satisfactorily described without taking into account patterns in performance. Several syntactic phenomena cannot be satisfactorily described without reference to performance-based factors, because their linguistic functions are intertwined with specific social, situational, and communicational contexts. One of these phenomena is the [V *until* ADJ]-construction as in 'Fry until crisp' or 'Whisk until smooth'. Based on an investigation of a section of the *Corpus of Contemporary American English*, the study takes into account empirically observed internal and external patterns of usage in the description of this construction and provides a usage-based constructional overview of the competence pertaining to [V *until* ADJ]. Jensen aims to provide a communicatively and cognitively plausible account of this particular phenomenon and to show that no satisfactory description of the construction which ignores performance-based data would be possible. This is because the construction itself is very much defined by external properties such as specific genre and register affiliations and a quite specific communicative function.

Linguistic Competences: Do they really need improving? by Anna Kristina Hultgren approaches the notion of 'linguistic competences' from a critical angle asking what people actually mean by 'linguistic competences' and why it apparently has become a central concept in contemporary society. It raises the question of whether it is always appropriate or helpful to accord linguistic competence with the attention that it seems to attract. It draws on examples from two contexts: the globalised call centers industry and the eight internationalised universities of Denmark. According to the European Commission, competences in other languages have come to be seen as highly important in the globalised world, which has become increasingly translingual, transcultural and transnational with extra pressure on making oneself understood. The paper finds that a strengthening of linguistic competences is hailed as the same solution to problems which are very different in nature and which are perceived to exist in both the call centers and the universities. Drawing on the notion of "verbal hygiene", it then proposes that the preoccupation with linguistic competences may be interpreted as a symbolic act for a much more fundamental urge of human being to put the world to right.

References

Bachman, Lyle F. 1990. *Fundamental Considerations in Language Testing.* Oxford: OUP.

Bachman, Lyle F. and Adrian S. Palmer. 1996. *Language Testing in Practice: Designing and Developing Useful Language Tests.* Oxford: OUP.

Bagari, Vesna, and Jelena Mihaljević Djigunović. 2007. Defining Communicative Competence. *Metodika* 8: 94-103.

Belmonte, Isabel Alonso; McCabe, Anne. 2004. The development of written discourse competence in ELT materials: a preliminary analysis. *Revista Canaria De Estudios Ingleses Volumen: 49.* Universidad de La Laguna.

Bruner, Jerome. 1983. *Child's Talk: Learning to Use Language.* New York: W. W. Norton and Company, Inc.

Bybee, Joan. 2010. *Language, Usage and Cognition.* Cambridge: Cambridge University Press.

Byram, Michael, Bella Gribkova and Hugh Starkey. 2002. *Developing the Intercultural Dimension in Language Teaching: a practical introduction for teachers.* Language Policy Division, Directorate of School, Out-of School and Higher Education, Council of Europe, Strasbourg. Leading Education and Social Research.

Byram, Michael. 2010. Linguistic and Cultural Education for Bildung and Citizenship. *The Modern Language Journal* 94(2): 317-321.

Byram, Michael. 1997. *Teaching and assessing intercultural communicative competence.* Clevedon: Multilingual Matters.

Canale, Michael. 1983. From communicative competence to communicative language pedagogy. In *Language and Communication,* edited by Jack C. Richards and Richard W. Schmidt, 2-27. London: Longman.

Canale, Michael. 1984. A communicative approach to language proficiency assessment in a minority setting. In *Communicative competence approaches to language proficiency assessment: Research and application,* edited by Charlene Rivera, 107-122. Clevedon: Multilingual Matters.

Canale, Merril and Merril Swain. 1980. Theoretical bases of communicative approaches to second language teaching and testing. *Applied Linguistics* 1: 1-47.

Canale, Michael and Merril Swain. 1981. A Theoretical Framework for Communicative Competence. In *The Construct Validation of Test of Communicative Competence,* edited by Adrian Palmer, Peter Groot and George Trosper, 31-36. Washington D.C.: TESOL.

CEF. Common European Framework of Reference for Languages. 2001: *Learning, Teaching, Assessment.* Council for Cultural Co-operation Educ. Committee, Modern Languages Division, Strasbourg. Cambridge: Cambridge UP/Council of Europe.

CEF. Common European Framework. 2005. *Acquiring Sociocultural Competence.* Council for Cultural Co-operation Educ. Committee, Modern Languages Division, Strasbourg. Cambridge: Cambridge UP/Council of Europe.

Chomsky, Noam. 1965. *Aspects of the Theory of Syntax.* Cambridge, Massachusetts: The MIT Press.

Diller, Jerry, Jean Moule, J. 2005. *Cultural Competence.* Portland, OR: Book News.

Ellis, Rod. 1997. *SLA Research and Language Teaching.* Oxford: Oxford University Press.

Ellis, Rod. 2008. *The Study of Second Language Acquisition.* Oxford: Oxford University Press

Gass, Susan; Selinker, Larry. 2008. *Second Language Acquisition: An Introductory Course.* New York: Routledge.

Goldberg, Adele. 2006. *Constructions at Work: The Nature of Generalization in Language.* Oxford: Oxford University Press.

Hymes, Dell. 1972. On Communicative Competence. In *Sociolinguistics: Selected Reading,* edited by J.B. Pride and Janet Holmes, 269-293. Harmondsworth: Penguin.

Kramsch, Claire. 2010. Plenary speeches: The symbolic dimensions of the intercultural. *Language Teaching* 44: 354–67.

Kramsch, Claire, and A. Whiteside. 2008. Language ecology in multilingual settings towards a theory of symbolic competence. *Applied Linguistics* 29, no. 4: 645–71.

Langacker, Ronald. 1987. *Foundations of Cognitive Grammar, vol. 1.Theoretical Prerequisites.* Stanford: Stanford University Press.

Langacker, Ronald. 1991. *Foundations of Cognitive Grammar, vol. II. Descriptive Application.* Stanford: Stanford University Press.

Leung, Constant & Jo Lewkowicz. 2013. Language communication and communicative competence: a view from contemporary classrooms. *Language and Education,* 27:5,398-414.

Montalt Ressurrecció, Vicent; Pilar. Ezpeleta Piorno; Isabel. García Izquierdo.2008. Developing communicative and Textual Competence through Genres. *Translation Journal,* 12 (4). (http://translationjournal.net/jounal/46competence.htm, accessed May 2014).

Paradis, Carita. 2003. Is the notion of *linguistic competence* relevant in Cognitive Linguistics? *Annual Review of Cognitive Linguistics* 1: 207-231. Amsterdam: John Benjamins Publishing Company.

Seidl, Monica.1998. Language and culture: towards a transcultural competence in language learning. *Forum for Modern Language Studies (OUP), Special Issue 1998: Language Teaching in Higher Education: Trends and Perspectives,* 101-113.

Tomasello, Michael. 2003. *Constructing a Language: A Usage-Based Theory of Language Acquisition.* Cambridge, MA: Harvard University Press.

Correlation between theoretical knowledge of grammar and performance and performance in the production of written texts

Richard Madsen

Abstract
This paper is a case study of the performance of my students of English language. I quantify, analyse and compare their results in an exam of theoretical grammar and their written home assignments. As my immediate goals, I attempt to identify problematic areas in my students' acquisition of English and to draw up some suggestions to improve courses in the future. As my extended goal, I consider the role and potential of teaching theoretical grammar in order to facilitate language acquisition.

Introduction and theory
This paper is a report of my analysis of my students' performance in the subjects English Grammar, and Production of Written Genres. The students involved are freshmen of English Business Communication at the University of Aalborg, Denmark in the academic year 2012-2013.

This is a pilot study in a larger project whose goal is to investigate Danish students' acquisition of English, including but not limited to what difficulties the students encounter in the process of acquisition. Thus, the primary goal of this analysis is to gain in-depth knowledge of status quo, i.e. how far my students have advanced in their acquisition of English and which areas of English pose the greatest difficulties to them. The results of this pilot study will provide a starting point for my further research. For this reason, the study at hand is mainly inductive.

Another purpose of this study is to see whether there is a correlation between knowledge of theoretical grammar and actual performance in the production of written texts, that is, a correlation between knowing grammar and being able to use it. The reason for doing this analysis is twofold. One is practical: I teach the same group of students both theoretical grammar and practical writing skills. Therefore, I am as their teacher interested in knowing whether students who do well in one of the subjects also do well in the other one, or whether there is some bias in their performance in these two subjects. The other – related –reason is that I would like to do some preliminary tests on claims concerning second/foreign language acquisition (SLA), English being my students' second/foreign language.

Researchers of SLA have conflicting views as to the usefulness of teaching theoretical grammar with the purpose of facilitating the acquisition of a second/foreign language. Researchers who believe in the Chomskyan Language Acquisition Device (Chomsky 1965) tend to think that teaching theoretical grammar has very little, if any, influence on acquiring the new language, i.e. it is useless for the purpose of facilitating acquisition (Krashen 1981, 1982).

On the other hand, teachers of foreign languages have for centuries taught theoretical grammar, more or less tacitly assuming that it is useful, even necessary for acquiring a new language. The so-called grammar and translation method (Rod 2012, Saville-Troike 2012), which is in fact one of the methods used in our very department inasmuch translation is one of the skills trained, is an example par excellence of this opinion.

The view that knowing theoretical grammar is useful is also embraced by e.g. Byram et al. (2009), and it is also institutionalised in the curriculum of Danish grammar schools[1] in the form of the multidisciplinary course General language understanding, essentially a scaled-down course in linguistics, whose purpose is to raise pupils' language awareness in order to improve their acquisition of foreign languages (taught in separate courses). For an overview in English see STX 2013, for details in Danish see Almen sprogforståelse 2013. Only grammar schools offer this course; other types of secondary schools do not.

By comparing how well my students do in theoretical grammar and how well they write English, I can provide some preliminary insights into the usefulness of teaching theoretical grammar with the purpose of facilitating the acquisition of a second language.

Building upon the analyses of my students' performance, my tertiary purpose is to come up with some preliminary, yet informed suggestions as for fine-tuning the courses I teach as well as the exams administered in order better to promote the students' acquisition of English.

Method
The method of this study is highly inductive in nature as I base my study on error analysis, i.e. the classification and counting of the mistakes the students have made in various tasks (Corder 1987). The data collected from the error analysis are then subjected to statistical analysis as described below. Table 1 below gives an overview of my research objectives.

---

[1] Called gymnasium in much of Continental Europe, i.e. secondary schools whose purpose is to provide generic education and prepare for college and university. In Danish nomenclature, such schools are referred to with the abbreviation stx.

Table 1: Research objectives

Areas of scrutiny	
(A) my students' knowledge of theoretical English grammar	**(B)** my students' practical grammar skills in writing
(C) whether there is a correlation between (A) and (B), i.e. whether there is a correlation between knowledge of theoretical grammar and possessing skills to write grammatically correct texts	
	(D) whether my students have improved their writing skills during their first year of study

For (A), I quantify students' knowledge of different areas of theoretical English grammar as displayed in the various tasks in their grammar exam. For (B) I make an extensive error analysis of my students' writings in different genres. I am also interested in whether any difference in my students' achievement can be ascribed to sex or educational background. (C) is then essentially a comparison of the analyses in (A) and (B).

As for (C), my underlying assumption is – as alluded to in the Introduction – that students who know the grammar of English better are also better at putting this knowledge to use, i.e. they write English better. I intend to find out whether this assumption bears out or is merely the wishful thinking of the grammar teacher.

For (D) I compare my students' writings in the spring semester with those in the autumn semester to see whether they show improvement in their writing skills.

The analysis pertaining to (A) is presented in the section Analysis of the grammar exam whereas the analyses pertaining to (B), (C) and (D) are presented in the section Analysis of the PWG assignments.

The study at hand is heavily statistical, and statistics is usually used to make claims about large populations based on the analysis of relatively small samples. (All my statistical calculations and considerations are based on Baayen 2008, Hatch and Hussein 1982, Rumsey 2011, 2012, and Urdan 2012.) Hence, it would be fair to expect that I would make claims about students of English in general.

However, general statistical claims are only valid if the samples are random. Arguably, my students were assigned to me randomly. However, I, the teacher, am also in the equation, and I am not random – in the sense that I have influenced all my students and have not influenced any of my colleagues' students. And since my samples are drawn only from the population of my students, I have – arguably – contaminated them beyond repair.

On the other hand, my data were collected before I even thought of making this study, as my data are the works of my students, which I gather routinely semester after semester as part of my teaching and assessment of the students, and I first started to think of a possible analysis of these data after the courses finished in the spring of 2013. Therefore, my teaching was not affected by the goals of the analysis.

Furthermore, even if my analysis might not be generalizable to other students of English with respect to details of the analysis, it is still valid with respect to the overall goal, which is to shed light on the relationship between knowing grammar consciously and using it subconsciously. Thus, for instance, if my colleagues emphasized pronouns in their teaching more than I did, it is expectable that their students' knowledge and use of pronouns is better than my students' knowledge and use of pronouns, i.e. a difference between these groups of students in detail. However, the relationship between the knowledge of and the use of pronouns – and those of other areas of grammar – is likely to show the same tendencies across different groups of students.

Hence I believe that my analysis is a valid way of addressing the issues drafted in the introduction and can thus also be interesting for other practitioners and theoreticians, not only me myself.

Data

I have – as mentioned above – collected data from freshmen of English Business Communication, whom I taught the courses English Grammar (theoretical subject) and Production of Written Genres (practical subject) in both the first (autumn) and second (spring) semester of the academic year 2012-2013. In both courses I taught the same two classes of altogether 58 students. They form my population and constitute half of the freshmen that started in English Business Communication in 2012. The courses are described in more detail below.

The course English grammar

The curriculum of English Grammar in the first semester comprises basic English morphology and syntax. Reading material in the first term was Madsen 2012; in the second term chapters 4-8 in Hjulmann and Schwartz 2012. Both books cover the same areas of English grammar; the difference is that Madsen is written in Danish and is much more detailed than Hjulmann and Schwartz. The intention was to use Madsen in both semesters; however, its high level of detail was criticised by both students and colleagues; thus we switched to a simpler text book in the second term.

The first semester ends with a written exam. The results of this exam constitute one set of my data. The exam consists of 100 questions divided into 14 topics as summarised in Table 2. The exam itself can be found in Appendix A.

Table 2: Topics of the grammar exam

Topics	Number of questions per topic
parts of speech	11
semantic relations	3
morphological analysis	1
clause constituents	20
clause vs. phrase	10
phrase types	10
phrase constituents	10

Topics	Number of questions per topic
pronoun types	10
subclause types	7
subclause finiteness	7
verb finiteness	1
independent clauses in a period	5
comma in connection with relative clause	4
choice of relative pronoun	1

The questions are usually presented in the form of a sentence in which a certain sequence is underlined, and the students have to provide an answer relevant for the given topic – e.g. what clause constituent the underlined sequence of words is. The students are not required to explain or describe any grammatical rules. Every correct answer yields one point; hence, the students can score at most 100 points. Less than 60 points means failing the exam.

In the second semester, the syllabus is extended with a fairly detailed discussion of verbs and verb phrases, but no exam such as in the first term is administered. Consequently, the metrics of my students' knowledge of theoretical grammar is entirely their achievement at the exam in the first term.

Because I measure the students' performance in Production of Written Genres in terms of mistakes committed (see below), so do I their performance in English Grammar. Hence, my data set actually contains the number of wrong answers they had in their exams: anything between 0 and 100, where 0 is of course the best, and more than 40 means failure.

The course Production of Written Genres
In this course, henceforth PWG, the students are trained in writing summaries, translation of texts from Danish into English, and free writing of texts on a set topic. The text of free writing and the summary have a preset limit on the maximum number of words the students are allowed to write. For free writing, it is 300 words; for summary, it is 20% of the original text, 270 words in the autumn and 185 words in the spring. There is

no preset limit for translation. There is also no lower limit on the number of words in any of the text types.

Besides the different writing tasks, the students are also introduced to topics such as semantic relations, text types, communication model, cohesion, politeness and formality. The reading material is Albrecht 2010, Buhl 2005, ch. 5 in Björk and Räisänen 2003 and ch. 2 in Baker 1992.

In both semesters, the students have to hand in one assignment within each of the three types of tasks mentioned above. Hence, I have one free writing, one summary and one translation from every student in both semesters, totalling six texts per student – at least ideally since some, luckily only few, students have forgotten to hand in some of their assignments. The semesters are assessed separately so that I can also measure whether their writing has improved from the first to the second semester.

Only the assignments prescribed in the second semester constitute the exam in PWG, which is a portfolio exam. Nevertheless, the assignments are administered in the same way in both semesters and thus provide fully comparable data sets.

Each assignment is corrected by me, the teacher, in the way that I classify every mistake a student makes into one of 30 predefined types of errors (see Table 3). I annotate the students' documents with comments in their files. An example of such an annotated assignment can be seen in Appendix B. It is then at the end of the second term the task of the students to correct their texts according to my hints. The corrected texts from the second semester also form part of the students' evaluation; however, these are not analysed in this study. Hence, only the original assignments enter my data set.

For each student, my data sets contain a count of all their mistakes sorted into the predefined types of errors mentioned just above and stored in an MS Excel file. The collection of data was done by subroutines written in MS Visual Basic for Applications. The statistical calculations were done in MS Excel.

Since the number of words that a given assignment contains varies from student to student and from genre to genre, my data set contains the counts of errors divided by the number of words in the actual text. In this way, it is possible to fairly compare the students with one another as well as the text types with one another. In order to ease reading the figures, they are all scaled up by 100; that is, the actual numbers express the number of mistakes per 100 words.

It must be noted that there is a slight difference in the mathematical nature between the data sets. The data set of English Grammar is closed in the sense that it is only possible to commit at most 100 mistakes. On the other hand, the data sets of PWG are open-ended since it is – at least in principle – possible to commit any number of mistakes in a text; for instance, a word or expression can be faulty in several ways at the same time, and any number of punctuation marks can be faulty or missing irrespective of how many words are present in a text.

I have divided the error types into three groups: (gram) errors of grammatical nature, (sem) errors of semantic or pragmatic nature, and (orto) orthographical errors. Table 3 below summarises the error types.

Table 3: Types of errors

Abbr.	Brief description of the scope of the error (the abbreviations are based on Danish grammar terminology because the same set of abbreviations are also used in non-English courses in our department)	Type
ADJF	Adjective	gram
AF	Article	gram
ASF	Aspect	gram
BEGF	Capitalisation	orto
BF	Inflection	gram
DF	Derivation	gram
DIF	Voice	gram
GF	Choice of word	sem
GNF	Genitive	gram

Abbr.	Brief description of the scope of the error (the abbreviations are based on Danish grammar terminology because the same set of abbreviations are also used in non-English courses in our department)	Type
IF	Idiom	sem
KF	Agreement	gram
KONF	Structure	gram
MF	Modality	gram
MIF	Misunderstanding	sem
NF	Number	gram
OF	Translation	sem
OKF	Part of speech	gram
OSF	Constituent order	gram
PF	Pronoun	sem
PRF	Preposition	gram
RPF	Relative pronoun	gram
SF	Style	2
SMF	Cohesion	sem
SSF	Compounding	orto
STVF	Spelling	orto
SUBF	Noun	gram
TF	Tense	gram
TSF	Punctuation	orto
UF	Omission (either something that is supposed to be present but is omitted, or something that is present but should be omitted)	3
VF	Verb	gram

2   Instances of stylistic error are individually subclassified into the three superordinate error types.
3   Such errors are left unclassified. This error type is only used when none of the other error types fits, e.g. when the country code in a telephone number is forgotten in an assignment which purports to be a business letter.

Arguably, there is overlap between the error types, so some mistakes in the students' texts might be classified into several error types. I have always assigned a given mistake to one and only one error type; however, I dare not swear that I have always done so consistently. Therefore, I have not attempted to correlate individual error types with individual topics in the grammar exam (see above). On the other hand, whenever one expression contains several distinct mistakes, I have counted all the corresponding error types.

For example, *BP **are owning** several refineries* features both an agreement error in the given context and an aspect error; thus, I have counted two mistakes, one of each type.

Background information
Apart from the grammar exam and the writing assignments described above, I have also collected the following pieces of background information on my students via a questionnaire in order to see if these factors have any bearing on the students' performance: age, sex/gender, type of secondary education, languages acquired by the students in their childhood, amount of time spent abroad working or studying, and other languages spoken. For ensuing studies, I contemplate on collecting information on further socio-economic and motivational factors.

The overwhelming majority of my students, about 90%, turned out to only have acquired Danish in their childhood, and to never have spent time abroad working or studying. They are also very close to one another age-wise: average age at the grammar exam 22.03 years with a standard deviation of only 2.02. Only about 25% of them claimed to know any other languages than Danish and English, which is very strange since a second foreign language is taught to almost everyone from grade 7 onwards. Since there is very little variation concerning age and linguistic background, only the information on sex and secondary education is used in my further analysis.

Figure 1 shows the distribution of secondary education.[4]

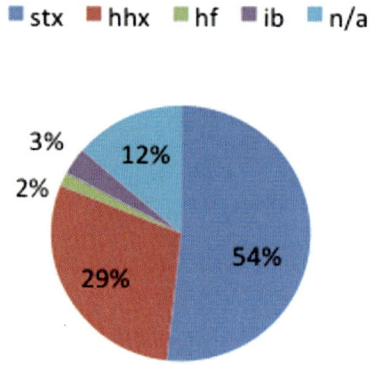

Figure 1 Secondary education

Since the numbers of hf and ib students are not even close to 30, which is considered the preferred lower limit on the number of informants (Urdan 2012, Kindle Location 1561-1577, "The Central Limit Theorem", Chapter 6), and are also a magnitude lower than the number of the stx and hhx students, I consider these groups negligible and make further calculations only on the stx and hhx groups.

---

4   Stx: 3-year grammar school; hhx: business school; ib: international business school; hf: 2-year grammar school; n/a: unknown. See Overview of the Danish education system 2013.

Analysis of the grammar exam

Table 4 summarises the results of the grammar exam. Remember that I measure performance in terms of mistakes, so less is better. Thus, female students seem to have done better than male students, and hhx students seem to have outperformed stx students.

Table 4 Statistical overview of the grammar exam

	N	Average number of wrong answers	Standard deviation	Median	Number of failees	Percentage of failees in the whole population	Percentage of failees within the sample
Whole population	58	32.21	16.31	29.0	17	29.31%	-
Females	35	29.71	13.53	28.0	7	12.07%	20.00%
Males	23	36.00	19.83	39.0	10	17.24%	43.48%
Stx	31	29.81	14.45	28.0	7	12.07%	22.58%
Hhx	17	27.77	14.52	24.0	3	5.17%	17.65%

The difference between stx and hhx students is according to Student's t-test insignificant at $p=0.64$; i.e. there is a 64% probability that the measured difference is merely accidental. Consequently, I conclude that my students' high-school background does not matter with respect to their learning theoretical grammar. Nevertheless, it is surprising that hhx students seem to outperform stx students. It counters my colleagues' and my expectations since stx is supposed to give a better training in languages. This matter deserves further investigation.

In purely statistical terms, nor is the difference between female and male students significant at p=0.19 (Table 4). However, it does raise concern in my mind that not only is the average performance of male students markedly worse than that of female students, but also that male students supply more than half of the re-examinandi even though they make up only about a third of the student population. This is well reflected in both their mean and median, which are awfully close to 40, which is the threshold between pass and fail. In addition, variance (as indicated by the standard deviation) is noticeably higher among the male students than among the female students, suggesting that the male students are a more heterogeneous group.

Figure 2 shows how well the students performed within the individual topics of the grammar exam. Sex and secondary education are not taken into account here. Again, lower is better.

Figure 2 Topics in the grammar exam

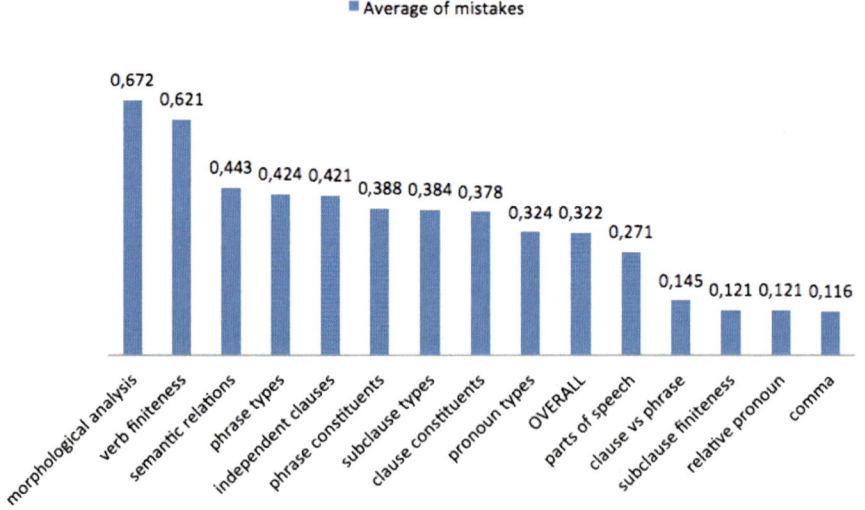

Since the topics sport a variable number of questions (see overview in the section The course English grammar), I have normalised the students'

averages to between 0 and 1 so that the topics can be compared with one another.

It is interesting to note that three of the topics the students did best at, clause vs. phrase, subclause finiteness and comma (with relative clauses), comprise questions with only two possible answers, which are moreover stated in the topic questions, such as *Is the underlined sequence of words a phrase or a clause?* Perhaps the students ought to be given a little more challenge in future exams by open questions, such as *What is the underlined sequence of words?*

Especially, their very good performance at the comma topic in the grammar exam is at odds with their lacking ability to use punctuation properly in their written assignments, in which punctuation mistakes – largely due to misplaced commas – are the most "popular" error type (see Analysis of the PWG assignments below). Perhaps the students' awareness could be stimulated by an open question such as *Where would you – if anywhere – place comma in the sentences below?*

As for finiteness, it is worth noting the large discrepancy between the related topics verb finiteness (the second worse) and subclause finiteness (the third best). In the latter, the students have to determine whether a given subclause is finite or non-finite, with these two possibilities being given in the question. In the former, they have to determine which ones on a list of verb forms are (non-)finite: e.g. *Which of the following verb forms are finite: gerund, subjunctive, present tense, infinitive, past participle?* The students' very poor accomplishment with this task suggests that they have little idea what the grammatical terms in the question refer to. This lack of knowledge may impede their development in the second semester, in which the verb phrase is the main theme.

Last but not least, morphological analysis seems a disaster. Morphology had not been of high priority in the curriculum so far. The textbook Madsen 2012 is the first of the textbooks used in the last eight years that discusses morphology at length, and the grammar exam being analysed here is the first one within the last eight years to contain a question about morphology: the students have to analyse a complex word, such as *incontrovertibly*, in terms of roots and affixes. In my opinion, it is very important to raise the students' awareness of word structures because it can promote their acquisition of vocabulary, too. In view of the large number of mistakes with words in their written assignment (see next section), this issue merits some consideration.

To sum it up, I think the exams in the future should focus a little more on morphology, semantic relations, and avoid asking yes/no-type questions, all this in order to raise the students' awareness about both grammar and vocabulary. Some of these suggestions have already been incorporated in the exam in the autumn of 2013; however, I have not yet been able to assess the effects.

Analysis of the PWG assignments

In this section, I provide an analysis of the written assignments *per se*, their correlation with the grammar exam, and whether my students show signs of development.

Analysis of error types

First, Figure 3 provides an aggregate overview of the error types as drawn from every single assignment delivered by my students during the course of both semesters. Altogether, my students have written 76321 words and committed 4356 mistakes along the way, yielding an average of 5.71 mistakes per hundred words. The most prominent error type is by far punctuation, making up 20.91% of all mistakes. 75% of these mistakes have to do with the use of the comma; that is, mistakes concerning the comma comprise about 15% of all mistakes.

The next two most frequent error types, which together constitute 22.92% of all mistakes, have to do with vocabulary. This is one of the reasons why I argue in the section about the grammar exam that the students' awareness of vocabulary – together with morphology – ought to be elevated. A related error type, that of parts of speech (OKF), even adds 2.02 percent points more to this issue.

Another thing that deserves attention is the error types KF and GNF, which together make up 6.80% of all mistakes. It may not seem much; however, the problem is that these error types cover elementary grammatical phenomena such as subject-verb agreement and the formation of the genitive. I find it surprising that having been taught English for 9-10 years before entering the university, the students still make so many of these types of mistakes.

According to Slabakova 2010:244 as cited by Saville-Troike (2012: Kindle Locations 1571-1573) "It follows that in order to acquire meaning in an L2, the learner has to go through the inflectional morphology, and hence, morphology is the bottleneck of acquisition...Phrasal and linguistic pragmatic meaning comes for free!". This suggestion seems to corroborate my finding that morphology should be emphasized more in the teaching than hitherto.

Figure 3 Error types

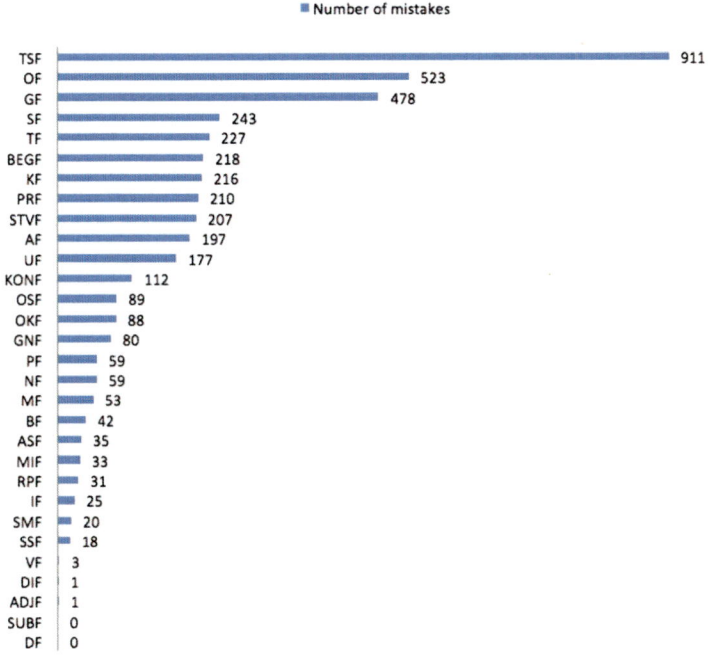

Sex and secondary education

As with the grammar exam, I also examine differences between subgroups of students with respect to sex and secondary education.

The number of informants varies from assignment to assignment since not all students handed in all three assignments. The three types of written assignments are analysed separately, and for each I make the calculations both for the total number of mistakes and for the mistakes of grammatical nature alone (see section The course Production of Written Genres about this distinction).

The results are tabulated in Table 6 and 7.

Table 6: Overall statistics of errors in the PWG assignments

		n	Mean	Median	Stddev
Free writing	errors/100 words	54	3.157	2.795	1.864
	grammatical errors/100 words		0.963	0.895	0.805
Summary	errors/100 words	57	4.227	4.444	1.976
	grammatical errors/100 words		1.177	0.816	1.037
Translation	errors/100 words	57	9.244	8.982	3.233
	grammatical errors/100 words		2.767	2.346	1.470

Table 7: Differences with respect to gender in the PWG assignments

		Women				Men				p
		n	Stddev	Median	Mean	Mean	Median	Stddev	n	
Free writing	errors/100 words	32	1.624	2.433	2.871	3.573	3.450	2.176	22	0.206
	gr.errs/100 words		0.715	0.895	0.914	1.035	0.928	0.950		0.616
Summary	errors/100 words	34	2.075	3.768	3.942	4.648	4.490	1.830	23	0.182
	gr.errs/100 words		1.105	1.113	1.251	1.069	0.784	0.967		0.515
Translation	errors/100 words	34	3.304	9.062	9.500	8.866	8.982	3.232	23	0.475
	gr.errs/100 words		1.708	2.517	3.052	2.346	2.286	0.957		0.051

As can be seen, female students tend to do a little better in free writing and summarising whereas male students seem better at translating. Nevertheless, the differences are not significant in any of the cases according to the t-test as the p-value is always higher than 0.05 although it comes very close to it in the case of grammatical errors in translation. I.e. male students seem to make markedly fewer grammatical mistakes in translation than female students.

Table 8: Differences with respect to secondary education in the PWG assignments

		hhx				stx				p
		n	Stddev	Median	Mean	Mean	Median	Stddev	n	
Free writing	errors/100 words	18	1.948	2.535	3.108	3.076	2.924	1.725	29	0.954
	gr.errs/100 words		0.766	0.944	0.800	1.101	0.971	0.837		0.214
Summary	errors/100 words	17	1.631	3.802	3.757	4.160	4.183	2.081	31	0.463
	gr.errs/100 words		0.858	0.760	0.949	1.092	0.784	0.934		0.597
Translation	errors/100 words	18	2.898	8.971	8.746	8.998	8.741	2.880	30	0.772
	gr.errs/100 words		1.035	2.517	2.728	2.562	2.156	1.389		0.640

The difference between hhx and stx students is in all the assignments insignificant, and – as opposed to the grammar exam – not always to the hhx students' advantage (see Table 8).

Correlation analysis

Table 9 sums up the results of the correlation analysis of the grammar exam and the written assignments in the autumn semester.

Table 9: Correlations between knowledge of theoretical grammar and practical grammar skills

Autumn semester: grammar vs. PWG		n	Mean	Median	Stddev	r⁵
Free writing	words (max. 300)	54	221.204	222.5	44.193	-0.209
	errors/100 words		3.157	2.795	1.864	0.279
	grammatical errors/100 words		0.963	0.895	0.805	0.300
Summary	words (max. 270)	57	259.737	267	18.757	-0.016
	errors/100 words		4.227	4.444	1.976	0.444
	grammatical errors/100 words		1.177	0.816	1.037	0.252
Translation	words	57	348.292	348	22.179	-0.312
	errors/100 words		9.244	8.982	3.233	0.550
	grammatical errors/100 words		2.767	2.346	1.470	0.242

First a few general comments: Clearly, the students have least trouble with the free-writing assignment; then comes the summary assignment, and translation is the most troublesome. It is probably no surprise. In free writing, one can easily avoid those constructions which are not familiar, and in summary, one can more or less copy and paste from the text that is being summarised. On the other hand, in translation, one is forced to follow the original text's lead and must try to convert it as faithfully as possible – of course within the limits of what feels natural in the target language – regardless whether one feels comfortable with the required constructions or not.

Interestingly, the students have written the shortest texts in free writing, where the average length of the texts is quite below the allowed maximum. On the other hand, they seem to have tried to approach the maximum as closely as possible in their summaries. Apparently, they believe a longer summary is better than a shorter one. Or they may find it difficult to reduce information.

---

5   Pearson's linear correlation coefficient, r, goes from -1 to +1. The closer it comes to ±1, the stronger is the correlation. Negative values indicate inverse correlation. Values close to 0 on either side indicate lack of linear correlation. Here, r shows the correlation between the achievement in the grammar exam and the performance in the various written assignments.

As for translation, which does not have a set limit on the number of words, there is an interesting effect. There seems to be a moderate correlation between the length of the translations and how good the writers are at English (r=-0.312). In other words, stronger students tend to write wordier translations, and weaker students tend to write more tersely.[6] A similar, though weaker, tendency seems to apply in the case of free writing, but no such correlation is detected in the case of summarising.

Turning to the correlation with the grammar exam, my hypothesis was that students who do better at the grammar exam also do better at the written assignments. This hypothesis is only partially borne out. The correlation is about moderate for summarising and rather weak for free writing. It is not strong for translation, either, though markedly stronger than for the other two types of assignment.

The difference between the correlations can probably be explained by alluding to what is already said above concerning the precision found in the different assignment types. Since it is easier to avoid mistakes in free writing and summarising, also for weaker students, the difference between strong and weak students evens out in these two tasks, but not so in translation.

Why the correlations are relatively low is explained by the apparently widespread existence of students who have a good command of English, but who have a limited conscious knowledge about it; and of students who know grammar, but who cannot put this knowledge to use when writing English. The chart in Figure 4 summarises these "deviant" students. Why there are relatively many students with biased knowledge remains to be investigated.

---

[6] The seemingly inverse correlation (negative r) is due to the fact that student strength is measured in number of mistakes made. Thus, fewer mistakes (stronger students) tend to correlate with longer translations, and more mistakes (weaker students) with shorter texts.

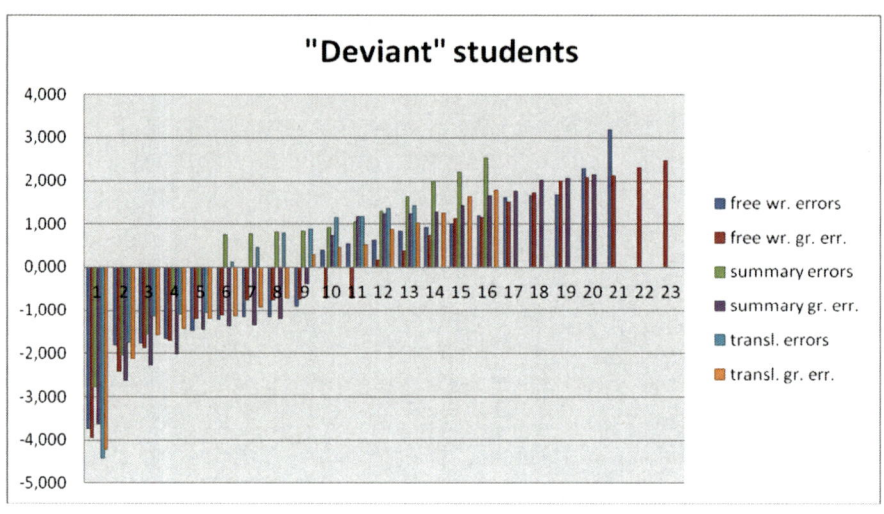

Figure 4 "Deviant" students

The chart shows two types of students: those who are above average in writing, but below average in theoretical grammar; and those who are below average in writing, but above average in theoretical grammar. Being below and being above average are both computed in terms of the respective standard deviations. The length of the bars shows the distance between a student's score in grammar and their score in a writing task, as measured in terms of standard deviations. By convention, positive bars indicate students who "favour" theoretical grammar, and negative bars indicate students who "favour" practical writing skills. The numbers on the horizontal axis simply indicate the number of "deviant" students, most in free writing, fewest in translation. They do not number or mark individual students, e.g. the number 2 does not indicate one particular person, but simply refers to the person(s) who happen(s) to be member number two in the respective groups.

Note that the bars merely indicate how far a student's knowledge of theoretical grammar is from their practical writing skills. The bars do not show anything about how strong or how weak a particular student is with respect to theoretical grammar or writing skills. Thus, the same positive bar could equally well indicate a student who is very good at grammar and slightly weak at writing, a student who is slightly good at grammar and very weak at writing, and anything in-between. In any case, long bars are indicative of "unideal" situations, i.e. students who have very biased knowledge.

What is really surprising is that the correlation of the grammatical error types alone is generally weaker in all three tasks than the correlation of all error types together (see Table 8). It is virtually non-existent in the case of summarising. It is contrary to what I expected, and I cannot provide a definitive explanation at this moment.

It seems to be the case that those students who are more grammar-aware – as shown by their results in the grammar exam – are even more aware of vocabulary than of grammar. It can also be an artefact of my particular division of the error types into grammatical and non-grammatical errors. A closer scrutiny of the data is required to elucidate the matter.

Development

This section is devoted to examining whether my students have improved from the autumn to the spring semester. Since there is no grammar exam in the spring term such as that in the autumn term, the measurement is based on my students' written assignments.

Unfortunately, my sizeable population of up to 58 students for the statistics performed above is now reduced to 30 odd for several reasons. Some students have quit (not unlikely due to their lack of success in grammar), some were reassigned to my colleagues for the spring semester and thus came out of my reach[7], and some failed to deliver one or more of their assignments. My statistics in this section are based only on those students who have delivered to me all their assignments in both semesters.

---

7   The idea of doing the present study arose in my mind towards the end of the semester. Because of this, I missed the opportunity to ask my colleagues to collect data, which would have required that they and I agree upon annotating the students' assignments in the same way.

Because the remaining informants are so few, I do not attempt to compare women with men or stx with hhx students. The subgroups would be too small for yielding meaningful statistics for my confidence.

I compute the development by dividing the number of each student's mistakes in the spring term with the corresponding number in the autumn term. If the number thus yielded is below 1, it indicates development, i.e. fewer mistakes made in the spring term than in the autumn term. Consequently, a number above 1 suggests lack of development, i.e. an increased number of mistakes made. Hence, as usual in this paper, lower is better. For instance, 0.8 means 20% amelioration; 1.2 means 20% deterioration.

A slight disadvantage of this method is that if one has 0 mistakes in the autumn, but some mistakes in the spring, then the division results in infinity and blows all the statistics. But since it is important to keep the measurement as proportionality because the students have different starting points, I must use division. So to circumvent the problem of infinity, I substitute for zero the next lowest number in the corresponding data subset from the autumn semester divided by two. Instead of making this calculation, I could have assigned an arbitrarily low number, say 0.000001, instead of zero. However, in this way, the students with zero errors are still credited with being the best in the class in the autumn at the task at hand, at the same time statistically allowing for the possibility that I may have overlooked a mistake or two in their assignments. In this way, their apparently dramatic decline is brought into a more realistic range.

Having computed the development coefficient for each student, I calculate – as usual – the relevant statistics, including significance levels with paired t-test, for the various types of assignments. The results are shown in Table 10.

Table 10: Development from autumn to spring

		n	Mean	Median	Stddev	p
	Mean difference between autumn and spring. Less than 1 indicates improvement					
Free writing	Errors/100 words	36	2.204	1.225	4.565	0.229
	Grammatical errors/100 words		2.038	1.129	2.945	0.189
Summary	Errors/100 words	35	1.328	1.092	0.887	0.184
	Grammatical errors/100 words		2.544	1.459	2.782	0.001
Translation	Errors/100 words	36	0.940	0.816	0.781	0.000
	Grammatical errors/100 words		1.296	0.986	1.287	0.751

It does not look good for free writing and summary; the students made considerably more mistakes in the spring than in the autumn. The increase in grammar mistakes in the summary is even statistically significant. Luckily, so is the slight improvement concerning the overall number of mistakes in translation.

One explanation that has been offered for the students' lack of improvement (David Carré and Brady Waggoner personal communication) is that the students have in fact expanded their knowledge during their first year at the university, but since this expansion is taxing on their cognitive resources, they have not yet been able to improve their precision. It requires further research to test this hypothesis.

Conclusion
As for the students' achievement in theoretical grammar, I showed that male students performed alarmingly poorly, only to some extent when compared to their female fellows, but to a large extent when compared to the requirements. However, I did not find any significant difference between the students with respect to their educational background. I also made some recommendations as to how the exam and curriculum could be modified in order to expedite the students' acquisition of English, such as emphasizing morphology in the curriculum and the avoidance of yes/no type questions in the grammar exam.

As for the students' performance in actual communication, I identified areas of major problems that the students have, e.g. punctuation, vocabulary and elementary grammar. I showed that there is no significant difference between the sexes and between different educational backgrounds, and concluded that my students made only limited if any improvement with respect to their precision in practical grammar skills.

As for the secondary goal of this study, that is to show if there is a correlation between knowledge of theoretical grammar and the ability to use grammar in writing, I deem it fairly conclusive. There does seem to be a sizeable proportion of students, 7 to 12 out of 58 (see Figure 4) who rather seem to conform to Krashen's monitor hypothesis (1981) insofar they are better than average at theoretical grammar while being below average in writing skills. In other words, they do not seem to be able to utilise their knowledge of theoretical grammar when communicating in English. Nevertheless, I did find weak to moderate correlation between my students' performance in theoretical and practical grammar, which seems to contradict Krashen's monitor hypothesis and related assumptions.

In any case, the students who do not show correlation between their knowledge of theoretical grammar and their ability to use grammar in communication deserve a closer examination.

References

Albrecht, Lone. 2010. *Textual Analysis and the Production of Text.* Samfundslitteratur.

Almen sprogforståelse. 2013. http://www.uvm.dk/Uddannelser-og-dagtilbud/Gymnasiale-uddannelser/Studieretninger-og-fag/Fag-paa-stx/~/media/UVM/Filer/Udd/Gym/PDF13/130405%20STX%20 Almen%20sprogforstaeelse%202010.ashx. Accessed 2013

Baayen, R. H. 2008. *Analyzing Linguistic Data: A Practical Introduction to Statistics using R.* Cambridge University Press.

Baker, Mona. 1992. *In Other Words. A coursebook on translation.* London: Routledge.

Björk, Lennart and Räisänen, Christine. 2003. *Academic Writing: A University Writing.* Lund, Studentlitteratur.

Buhl, Ole. 2005. *Oversættelse fra teori til praksis.* Hans Reitzels Forlag.

Byram, Michael S., Annette Søndergaard Gregersen, Anne Holmen, Karen Lund, Lars Stenius Stæhr, Birgit Henriksen and Merete Olsen. 2009. *Sprogfag i forandring: pædagogik og praksis.* Frederiksberg: Samfundslitteratur.

Chomsky, Noam. 1965. *Aspects of the Theory of Syntax.* MIT Press.

Corder, S. Pit. 1987. *Error Analysis and Interlanguage.* Oxford University Press.

Ellis, Rod. 2012. *Second Language Acquisition.* Oxford University Press.

Hatch, Evelyn and Farhady, Hossein.1982. *Research Design and Statistics for Applied Linguistics.* Newbury House Publishers, Rowley, Massachusetts.

Hjulmand, Lise-Lotte and Helge Schwarz. 2012. *A Concise Contrastive Grammar of English*. Frederiksberg: Samfundslitteratur.

Hjulmand, Lise-Lotte and Helge Schwarz. 2012. *A Concise Contrastive Grammar of English. Workbook*. Frederiksberg: Samfundslitteratur.

Jelen, Bill; Syrstad, Tracy. 2010. *VBA and Macros: Microsoft Excel 2010*. Pearson Education. Kindle Edition.

Keys, Kenny L. 2013. *Microsoft Word VBA Codes Are Easy to Learn Under an Hour for Some People*. Kindle Edition.

Krashen. Stephen D. 1981. *Second Language Acquisition and Second Language Learning*. University of Southern California

Krashen, Stephen D. 1982. *Principles and Practice in Second Language Acquisition*. University of Southern California.

Madsen, Richard. 2012. *Engelsk sprogbeskrivelse*. unpublished manuscript.

Overview of the Danish Education System. 2013. http://eng.uvm.dk/Education/Overview-of-the-Danish-Education-System. Accessed 2013.

Rumsey, Deborah. 2011. *Statistics For Dummies®*. John Wiley and Sons. Kindle Edition.

Rumsey, Deborah. 2012. *Statistics II for Dummies*. Wiley. Kindle Edition.

Saville-Troike, Muriel. 2012. *Introducing Second Language Acquisition*. Cambridge University Press. Kindle Edition.

STX. 2013. http://eng.uvm.dk/Education/Upper-Secondary-Education/Four-Upper-Secondary-Education-Programmes-in-Denmark/The-Gymnasium-(stx). Accessed 2013.

Urdan, Timothy C. 2012. *Statistics in Plain English*. Taylor and Francis. Kindle Edition.

Appendix A: Exam in theoretical grammar

Determine which part of speech the underlined words belong to. E.g. Grammar is exciting: noun. Here it suffices to only state the major parts of speech, so e.g. in the case of pronouns, it is enough to state 'pronoun', you do not have to be more specific and write say 'personal pronoun'.

1. This exam features John Maynard Keynes, who is one of the most famous <u>economists</u>.

2. This exam features John Maynard Keynes, who is one of the most <u>famous</u> economists.

3. This exam features John Maynard Keynes, who is one of <u>the</u> most famous economists.

4. This exam features John Maynard Keynes, who is one <u>of</u> the most famous economists.

5. This exam features John Maynard Keynes, <u>who</u> is one of the most famous economists.

6. This exam features John <u>Maynard</u> Keynes, who is one of the most famous economists.

7. This exam <u>features</u> John Maynard Keynes, who is one of the most famous economists.

8. His ideas found wide-spread use <u>after</u> he died.

9. It had <u>to</u> do with the economic situation after WWII.

10. Keynes was not only a scientist, <u>but</u> also a patron of the arts and an art collector.

11. His work is <u>highly</u> valued.

Determine the semantic relation between the expressions below. E.g. chair – furniture: chair is hyponym, furniture is hyperonym.

12. Cat vs. dog

13. Probability vs. likelihood

14. Linguistics vs. science

Divide the word below into root and affixes, and describe each morpheme. E.g. sleeplessness: sleep root, noun (nominal root); -less derivational suffix turning a noun into an adjective; -ness making a noun of an adjective.

15. Invariably

Determine what clause constituents the underlined sequences of words are. E.g. They esteem <u>their teacher</u>: DO

16. This exam features <u>John Maynard Keynes, who is one of the most famous economists</u>.

17. This exam <u>features</u> John Maynard Keynes, who is one of the most famous economists.

18. <u>This exam</u> features John Maynard Keynes, who is one of the most famous economists.

19. This exam features John Maynard Keynes, who is <u>one of the most famous economists</u>.

20. Keynes has given the study of economics <u>a tremendous contribution</u>.

21. Keynes has given <u>the study of economics</u> a tremendous contribution.

22. Specialists call his line of thinking <u>Keynesian economics</u>.

23. There are <u>several different branches of economics</u> nowadays.

24. <u>There</u> are several different branches of economics nowadays.

25. There are several different branches of economics <u>nowadays</u>.

26. <u>It</u> is not easy to decide which school of economics is the best.

27. It is <u>not</u> easy to decide which school of economics is the best.

28. It is not easy <u>to decide which school of economics is the best</u>.

29. <u>Whatever people say</u>, economics is complicated.

30. <u>Whatever</u> people say, economics is complicated.

31. Keynesians consider <u>it</u> a good idea that governments intervene in an economic crisis.

32. Keynesians consider it <u>a good idea</u> that governments intervene in an economic crisis.

33. Keynesians consider it a good idea <u>that governments intervene in an economic crisis</u>.

34. This view is, however, not shared <u>by all</u>.

35. You must abide <u>by the rules</u>.

Decide whether the underlined sequences of words are phrases or clauses:
E.g. She is <u>an adorable young woman</u>: phrase.

36. This exam features John Maynard Keynes, <u>who is one of the most famous economists</u>.

37. This exam features John Maynard Keynes, who is one <u>of the most famous economists</u>.

38. <u>Whatever people say</u>, economics is complicated.

39. Keynes has given the study of economics <u>a tremendous contribution</u>.

40. His ideas found wide-spread use <u>after his death</u>.

41. <u>Having attended Eton College</u>, Keynes studied at Cambridge University.

42. He had been interested in mathematics <u>since his early childhood</u>.

43. Keynes had a younger sister and <u>a younger brother</u>.

44. <u>If you're born in Cambridge</u>, you're expected to be clever.

45. I don't know <u>whether it goes for Oxford as well</u>.

Determine which phrase type the sequences of words below belong to. E.g. <u>the type of phrase</u>: NP.

46. a fellow economist

47. most famous

48. a

49. to this end

50. to learn

51. rather minor

52. someone special

53. the best

54. might have developed

55. even if

Determine what phrase constituent the underlined sequences of words are. E.g. in the most successful album by Rammstein: descriptor.

56. might have developed

57. might have developed

58. someone special

59. a fellow economist

60. a fellow economist

61. a fellow economist

62. several universities in the UK that are world-famous

63. several universities in the UK that are world-famous

64. several universities in the UK that are world-famous

65. more than likely

Determine what kind of pronoun the underlined words are. E.g. You should not doubt your abilities: possessive.

66. Everybody is dependent on money.

67. For <u>it</u> makes the world go round.

68. I wonder <u>who</u> has developed the concept of money.

69. The person by <u>whom</u> it was invented has been cursed by the poor and worshipped by the rich.

70. But money in <u>itself</u> is neither benign nor malign.

71. It can only exert <u>its</u> power through humans.

72. Unfortunately, they are even willing to kill <u>each other</u> for it.

73. Most people disapprove of <u>that</u> kind of viciousness, though.

74. Some have even claimed that only those who don't have <u>any</u> money can be really happy.

75. However, <u>nobody</u> in my circles subscribes to this view.

Determine the type of the underlined subclauses, i.e. adverbial, nominal, modifying. E.g. I have no idea <u>what type it may be</u>: nominal clause.

76. <u>Even though he came from the middle class</u>, Keynes mingled well with the upper class.
    nominal ☐   modifying ☐   adverbial ☐

77. Is the underlined subclause in (76) finite or non-finite?
    finite ☐   non-finite ☐

78. <u>Attending Eton College</u> is considered a privilege.
    nominal ☐   modifying ☐   adverbial ☐

79. Is the underlined subclause in (78) finite or non-finite?
    finite ☐   non-finite ☐

80. Many men <u>having attended Eton</u> have become important figures in the UK.
    nominal ☐   modifying ☐   adverbial ☐

81. Is the underlined subclause in (80) finite or non-finite?
    finite ☐   non-finite ☐

82. <u>Why it's so great</u> is something of a mystery to me, though.
    nominal ☐   modifying ☐   adverbial ☐

83. Is the underlined subclause in (82) finite or non-finite?
    finite ☐   non-finite ☐

84. Keynes married a woman <u>who had a low social background</u>.
    nominal ☐   modifying ☐   adverbial ☐

85. Is the underlined subclause in (84) finite or non-finite?
    finite ☐   non-finite ☐

86. It is, however, told <u>that he was very happy with her</u>.
    nominal ☐   modifying ☐   adverbial ☐

87. Is the underlined subclause in (86) finite or non-finite?
    finite ☐   non-finite ☐

88. <u>Had she not had a miscarriage</u>, they would also have had a child.
    nominal ☐   modifying ☐   adverbial ☐

89. Is the underlined subclause in (88) finite or non-finite?
    finite ☐   non-finite ☐

90. Which of the verb forms listed below are finite?
    gerund ☐ past participle ☐ imperative ☐ present ☐ infinitive ☐

Determine how many independent clauses the periods below consist of.

91. Keynes was not only interested in women, but also courted men.

92. Yet he married a woman with whom he is said to have been happy.

93. However well you think you know someone, you might still be surprised.

94. Keynes has written quite a few books, and he was also active in social life.

95. Many say that he was a genius and has inspired other thinkers.

Relative clauses: Are commas necessary with the relative clauses below?

96. Statistics(,) which is the study of probability and distribution(,) is an important part of economics.
    Yes ☐   No ☐

97. Cambridge University(,) consisting of several colleges(,) is one of the oldest universities in the world.
    Yes ☐   No ☐

98. A person(,) who has mastered economics(,) is called an economist.
    Yes ☐   No ☐

99. There is also a newspaper(,) which bears that name.
    Yes ☐   No ☐

Insert the correct relative pronoun in the sentence below:

100. John Maynard Keynes, _____ parents survived him, died in 1946.

The physical punishment has an impacted on the children's behaviour, they gets aggressive. Parents who were spanked when they were children do the same to their children. They grew up with it, and therefore think it is the right way to tell their children that what they are doing is wrong. 90 % adults use the physical punishment because they believe that it is effective and at the same times gives the children discipline, but it only works in a short term.

Appendix B: Excerpt from a written assignment, a summary

Effects of forward lexical transfer on formality level as an L2 English competency

Jesper Bonderup Frederiksen

Abstract
Crosslinguistic research has been concerned with lexical transfer in L2 English and found that typology and psychotypology are important factors in the facilitation of transfer between languages. Also, research on cognates has shown that bilinguals translate cognates faster and more readily than non-cognates and indicated that cognates are processed differently from non-cognates in the bilingual mind. Although there is now an emerging field of word-choice research, a neglected area has been the effects of lexical crosslinguistic influence on formality, which in the case of L2 English seems particularly worthy of attention due to the special character of the English lexicon as a mixture of vocabulary of mainly Germanic and Latinate origin. Most English words that are cognates for Danish students are of Germanic origin, whereas most words that are cognates for Spanish students are of Latinate origin. Latinate words are associated with higher linguistic register than Germanic words. Therefore, this study sets out to investigate the hypothesis that Danish university students of L2 English choose a high proportion of English words of Germanic origin compared to Spanish university students of L2 English. The hypothesis is being tested through an experiment currently

in progress, and preliminary results indicate that Danish L2 English users choose a high proportion of Germanic words although it is too early to draw any conclusion until the experiment is completed.

Introduction
Crosslinguistic influence is no longer disregarded as a factor in foreign language acquisition and use. There was a period of time in the latter half of the previous century when the phenomenon received little attention from researchers who were very critical of anything that could be related to contrastive language analysis. In that period, it had become the fashion that foreign languages should be acquired as naturalistically as possible and without relation to learners' first languages. However, much empirical research has since confirmed that there are indeed benefits to be reaped from contrastive language analysis in language acquisition, and crosslinguistic influence has again become an important and developing field of study due to the work of Eric Kellerman, Batia Laufer, Terence Odlin, Håkan Ringbom, Scott Jarvis, and a number of other researchers.

The term crosslinguistic influence (CLI) is currently the generally used term mainly for what is also still referred to as language transfer, but CLI is more inclusive than the latter term. The prime reason for using the term CLI is that it covers not only both positive transfer and negative transfer (interference) but also e.g. avoidance due to the influence of learners' first languages.

The directionality of CLI can be categorized as *forward* (from L1 to a second or later acquired language), *reverse* (from a second or later acquired language to L1), or *lateral* transfer (between second and later acquired languages). CLI types can also be categorized according to the area of language knowledge/use as phonological, orthographic, lexical, semantic, morphological, syntactic, discursive, pragmatic, or sociolinguistic. (Jarvis and Pavlenko, 2008: 20ff).

As pointed out by Jarvis and Pavlenko (2008: 88), much lexical CLI research has been concerned with errors rather than with word choice in situations where several lexical alternatives exist. This paper, however, focuses on the possible effects of forward lexical transfer on formality level as a language competence in L2 English. More specifically, the purpose of this paper is to present the hypothesis, theoretical background and preliminary results of a study comparing the L2 English word choice of Danish and Spanish university students of English.

Hypothesis

This study aims to test the following hypothesis:

H1: Danish university students of English whose L1 is Danish use lexis of Germanic origin to a larger extent in L2 English than do Spanish university students of English whose L1 is Spanish.

Theoretical background

The following sections will present the theoretical considerations underlying the hypothesis, i.e. 1) the relationship between proficiency and typology, 2) psychotypology, 3) markedness and prototypicality, 4) the Germanic-Latinate nature of the English lexicon and linguistic register, and 5) cognates.

The relationship between proficiency and typology

The term *typology* is used when classifying languages for the purpose of comparison and also when searching for universals. Some languages are more similar than others, i.e. they can be classified as typologically less distant than others on the basis of their structural similarities, including morphological ones (e.g. Crystal 1997).

When the L1 and the L2 are typologically similar, more CLI is likely to occur, according to e.g. Ringbom (2007), who found more examples of CLI in the English exam papers of Swedish-speaking Finns than in those produced by Finnish-speaking Finns. Typological similarity to an L1 will generally facilitate acquisition of an L2, not least at early stages of learning. So, even though more examples of CLI were found in the English of

Swedish-speaking Finns, this does not mean that the number of errors was higher than in the English of Finnish-speaking Finns. On the contrary, Swedish-speaking Finns did better in the exam papers that Ringbom analysed. Interestingly, these two subject groups afford a rare opportunity to study and compare groups whose cultural conditions are similar, which should facilitate the isolation of linguistic influence.

The positive effects of typological similarity are indicated by the rankings of the top 25 countries in an English proficiency index[1], which shows that L2 English speakers in countries where the L1 is Germanic are more proficient than L2 English speakers in countries where the L1 is Latinate. It might be noted that Finland and Hungary are the only countries with non-Germanic L1s but higher proficiency than some Germanic-speaking countries and that Belgium is of course a special case in that there is a Germanic L1, Flemish, in the north and a Latinate L1, Belgian French, in the south. Otherwise, the countries at the top of the rankings all have Germanic L1s:

2012 EF English Proficiency Index rankings

Very high proficiency
1 Sweden
2 Denmark
3 Netherlands
4 Finland
5 Norway

High proficiency
6 Belgium
7 Austria
8 Hungary
9 Germany

---

[1] The EF English Proficiency Index measures English proficiency in 54 countries based on a sample of around 1.7 million adults. Proficiency bands are aligned to the Common European Framework of Reference (CEFR) and EF course levels. Further details of the index and explanations of measurements can be found at http://www.ef.com/epi.

10 Poland
11 Czech Republic
12 Singapore
13 Malaysia

Moderate proficiency
14 India
15 Switzerland
16 Slovakia
17 Pakistan
18 Spain
19 Portugal
20 Argentina
21 South Korea
22 Japan
23 France
24 Italy
25 Hong Kong

Psychotypology
Objective typological similarities between languages are obviously relevant when it comes to transferability, but a crucial factor in connection with CLI effects on L2 performance is what Kellerman (1983) termed psychotypology, i.e. how similar the languages are in the judgment of the L2 user.

Ringbom (2007: 24-26) distinguishes between *perceived* and *assumed* similarity: It is possible for CLI to occur because an L2 user has either perceived a similarity or merely assumes a similarity between two languages. The latter type of similarity is what may typically cause negative transfer in the form of errors insofar as it is not based on previous perception, whereas the former type is usually helpful to the L2 user.

Assumed similarity is helpful only to the extent that it corresponds to objective similarity, and the distinction between perceived and assumed similarity should not be confused with that between *objective* and *sub-*

jective similarity. As Jarvis and Pavlenko indicate when explaining perceived and assumed similarity, both perception and assumption of similarity are subjective processes in the mind of the L2 user that may or may not overlap with objective similarity:

> ... perceived and assumed similarities are not always mutually exclusive. In fact, they represent a set-subset relationship in that all perceived similarities are also assumed similarities, but not all assumed similarities are actually perceived. Both perceived and assumed similarities diverge from objective similarities to the extent that L2 users' judgments concerning the similarities between languages are incomplete or erroneous. (Jarvis and Pavlenko 2008: 179)

L2 forms that are perceived as different from L1 forms may even be avoided. Dagut and Laufer (1985) demonstrated how the psychotypological phenomenon of avoidance applies to Hebrew speakers in the case of English phrasal verbs, a particularly Germanic structure. Hebrew does not have phrasal verbs, and the subjects in their study showed a preference for English single-word verbs rather than phrasal verbs and in particular rather than figurative phrasal verbs. With Eliasson, Laufer later compared the Hebrew L2 English users with Swedish L2 English users and found that Swedes show no reluctance in using English phrasal verbs, even where their use was figurative (Laufer and Eliasson 1993). As Swedish, unlike Hebrew, does have phrasal verbs, this is a strong indication of the importance of typology and psychotypology in CLI.

In relation to the present study, the question is how psychotypology might affect Danish or Spanish L2 users of English. The smaller the actual typological distance between languages, the more scope there is for perceiving and subsequently assuming similarity. If a Danish L2 English user perceives a large number of syntactic, morphological and lexico-semantic similarities between Danish and English through language comprehension, she would be more inclined to assume similarity when producing L2 English. A Spanish L2 user of English, on the other hand, would likely perceive comparatively less similarity between Spanish and English, and as a result she would be more reluctant to make assumptions of similarity although there are many Spanish cognates in English that might contribute to her L2 proficiency.

Markedness and prototypicality
According to Kellerman (1983), another factor that may promote transferability is whether the meaning, structure or use of an L1 item is perceived as marked or prototypical. Following Jarvis and Pavlenko (2008), the two concepts will be dealt with as one factor here. If the meaning, use or structure of an L1 item is perceived as prototypical or unmarked, the L1 item is more prone to transfer. Kellerman had previously found that Dutch students were more likely to regard English translations of the Dutch verb *breken* by the English *break* as more acceptable in idioms where the meaning was close to the core meaning than in idioms where *breken* had a non-core meaning.

For L2 English users whose L1 is Germanic, this factor could promote the choice of Germanic cognate[2] synonyms in those cases where the meaning of the L1 word is perceived by the L2 user as prototypical. Conversely, L2 English users whose L1 is Latinate are faced with the obstacle to transfer that most general and thus early acquired English words are of Germanic origin. This may, on the one hand, deprive L2 English users whose L1 is Latinate of an L2 target for transfer in the early stages of learning because they have not yet learned a Latinate cognate synonym in English, and may, on the other hand, instil in them a general perception that English is typologically distant from their Latinate L1 because the core meanings of most of the basic words in their L1 have Germanic equivalents in English.

The Germanic-Latinate nature of the English lexicon and linguistic register
The English lexicon is special in the sense that etymologically it is mainly a mixture of words of Germanic and Latinate origin due to the historical

---

2   Cognates are words that share meaning and phonological/orthographical form in different languages.

development of the English language from Old English (Anglo-Saxon) to Present-Day English. Although English is a Germanic language, it has assimilated so many influences from Latinate languages, especially French and Latin, that modern English is characterized by an unusually wide range of vocabulary and synonyms:

> Prominent among the assets of the English language must be considered the mixed character of its vocabulary. English is classified as a Germanic language. That is to say, it belongs to the group of languages to which German, Dutch, Flemish, Danish, Swedish, and Norwegian also belong. It shares with these languages similar grammatical structure and many common words. On the other hand, more than half of its vocabulary is derived from Latin. Some of these borrowings have been indirect, a great many through French, some through the other Romance languages. As a result, English also shares a great number of words with those languages of Europe that are derived from Latin, notably French, Italian, Spanish, and Portuguese. All this means that English presents a somewhat familiar appearance to anyone who speaks either a Germanic or a Romance language. There are parts of the language which one feels one does not have to learn, or learns with little effort. (Baugh and Cable 1993: 9-10)

Differentiation of synonyms (including near-synonyms) may sometimes be conceptual, as e.g. in the case of *ox* and *beef*, where the differentiation can be explained etymologically by the conceptual meaning of *ox* having already been established in the English lexicon when *beef* entered the language from French and *beef* thus acquiring its distinct reference to the meat of an ox (Smith 1996: 125). However, the English lexicon is characterized by numerous synonyms and near-synonyms where differentiation is not conceptual, but:

> ... differentiation can also take place with regard to associative (connotational and metaphorical) meaning. One good example of this process is to do with register-distinctions between native vocabulary and French-derived loanwords; it is 'felt' by

a speaker of Present-Day English that a French-derived word such as *commence* is somehow of a 'higher' register than *begin*, the latter being directly descended from Old English. (Smith 1996: 125)

In the many instances where English possesses synonyms and near-synonyms of Germanic and Latinate origin, respectively, word choice is therefore one of the factors that determine the formality level of a text. As Germanic vocabulary was present in the English lexicon before most Latinate words were assimilated and the assimilation of Latinate words historically occurred mainly through the higher echelons of society, there are, according to Baugh and Cable (1993: 182), a number of examples of modern English having a synonym or near-synonym at each of three levels: Popular (from Germanic), literary (from French), and learned (from Latin), such as e.g. the triplet *holy-sacred-consecrated*. It is very common to find examples in English of at least two synonyms where one is of Germanic origin and the other of Latinate origin. In these cases, the Latinate synonym is the more formal word, as can be seen in the examples listed below:

Germanic:	*Latinate:*
brotherhood	fraternity
help	assist
follow	pursue
drink	beverage
freedom	liberty
fall	decrease
begin	commence
deadly	mortal
put off	postpone
feel	sense

A simple comparison of the most frequent content words in the General Service List[3] (GSL) and the most frequent words in the Academic Word List[4] (AWL) provides an indication of the difference between Germanic and Latinate vocabulary in English in terms of linguistic register. Whereas Germanic words are predominant in general English, the majority of words in the AWL are of Latinate origin.

General Service List - 60 most frequent content words, ranked (West 1953)

9 have	58 year	79 even	100 just
31 would	60 take	80 find	102 good
33 will	61 come	81 day	105 feel
35 say	63 know	84 way	106 seem
37 make	64 see	85 many	108 high
39 can	65 use	86 must	109 too
40 more	66 get	87 look	110 place
43 man	67 like	89 great	111 little
45 other	69 first	92 long	112 world
48 time	71 work	93 where	113 very
50 go	72 now	94 much	114 still
54 could	73 may	95 should	115 nation
55 state	75 give	96 well	116 hand
56 only	77 think	97 people	117 old
57 new	78 most	99 own	118 life

---

3   The GSL is a list of about 2,284 words of general English vocabulary in order of frequency taken from a corpus of written English to represent the most frequent words of English for the benefit of ESL students and teachers. The GSL was created in 1953 by David West and updated (ranked by frequency and extended by 284 words) by John Bauman and Brent Culligan in 1995 based on the word frequencies in the Brown Corpus.
4   The AWL is a list of words which appear with high frequency in English-language academic texts. It was compiled on the basis of 3,500,000 words found in academic journals, textbooks, course workbooks, lab manuals, and course notes covering a range of academic subjects, and it includes neither technical terms specific to a certain field nor high-frequency general vocabulary.

Function words, for which there are rarely lexical alternatives, have been eliminated from this list to facilitate comparison with the AWL. The number in front of each word represents its original frequency rank in the GSL. The above list gives a clear indication of the predominance of Germanic vocabulary in general English.

Academic Word List - 60 most frequent words (Coxhead 2000)

analysis	established	occur
approach	estimate	percent
area	evidence	period
assessment	export	policy
assume	factors	principle
authority	financial	procedure
available	formula	process
benefit	function	required
concept	identified	research
consistent	income	response
constitutional	indicate	role
context	individual	section
contract	interpretation	sector
create	involved	significant
data	issues	similar
definition	labour	source
derived	legal	specific
distribution	legislation	structure
economic	major	theory
environment	method	variable

Only one word in the top 60 of the AWL, *income*, is of Germanic origin. According to Lubliner and Hiebert (2011) nearly 75% of all headwords in the AWL are in fact Spanish-English cognates.

One of the most detailed studies of the implications of Germanic versus Latinate vocabulary for linguistic register in English was conducted by Bar-Ilan and Berman (2007), who examined the proportion of Latinate words produced by L1 American English speakers in different age groups (4th graders, 7th graders, 11th graders and graduate-level university students) and in different text types (spoken narrative, spoken expository, written narrative and written expository). Their results showed a rise in the proportion of Latinate words with progressive age and also according to text types. Written language contained more Latinate words, and expository styles contained more Latinate words than did narrative styles. As their results provide support for the view that the lexicon is a crucial determinant of level of linguistic expression, they recommend using the distinction between Germanic and Latinate vocabulary as a criterion that can be applied more widely as a measure in linguistic analyses of English texts (Bar-Ilan and Berman 2007: 29).

As English has more levels of formality and stylistic registers than Danish due to the mixed lexical composition of the English language, there is the possibility that texts produced by Danish L2 English users could be perceived by native English speakers as less formal than intended by the sender as they might not correspond to the typical level of formality for the text genre concerned if, as a result of the lexical kinship between English and Danish, such texts contain more words of Germanic origin than would be expected in relatively formal text genres.

There is evidence that native speakers judge formality in relation to the proportions of Germanic and Latinate vocabulary. Levin and Novak (1991) found that undergraduates assigned a speaker to social categories (e.g. professor/employer, stranger, worker, acquaintance, close friend) depending on the proportions of Germanic and Latinate vocabulary used. They set out to test two factors that might explain judgments of formality: The frequency of a word in the English language and the historical status of a word due to Germanic/Latinate etymology. Their results showed that etymology was consistently a factor, i.e. Latinate words were judged more formal than Germanic words, whereas frequency was involved only in the case of Germanic words, which were judged more formal the lower their frequency in the language.

Taking the implications of lexical formality even further, in a study that involved analysing how listeners attributed personality traits to a speaker in relation to the proportions of Germanic and Latinate lexis used, Levin, Giles, and Garrett (1994) found that the lexical formality resulting from the proportions of Germanic and Latinate words in English texts correlates with recipients' attribution of personality traits to the sender:

> The marked formal style leads to many attributions to the speakers, many of them hardly flattering (such as ingratiating) but others, in line with the view that formal is encoded to create impressions of expertise, are favorably associated with notions of competence (Levin, Giles, and Garrett 1994: 265).

For example, they found that English speakers using Latinate lexis were judged to be more intelligent, dominant, and ambitious, but less sincere, old-fashioned, trustworthy, and sympathetic than English speakers using Germanic lexis.

> The trait assignments provide an overall impression that formal speakers are bright and competent, whereas their linguistically informal confreres are more vulnerable, likeable people (Levin, Giles, and Garrett 1994: 267).

In certain situations, there may of course be reasons for consciously choosing a lower rather than a higher level of lexical formality to facilitate comprehension. However, a low level of formality is problematic in so far as it is the inadvertent result of CLI due to lexical kinship between Germanic languages. If the frequency of English words of Germanic or Latinate origin affects recipient reactions in terms of trait attribution – as Levin, Giles, and Garrett conclude – lexical formality of Danish L2 English users is a linguistic dimension that could have social and communicative consequences and is worthy of more attention than it has received thus far.

Cognates

Cognates can be defined as words that share meaning and phonological/orthographical form in different languages. It is possible to distinguish between those that share a common etymology, having developed in different languages from the same historical root, and those that have been imported from a foreign language as loanwords (Serrander 2011: 27). In Danish, an example of the former type would be 'begynde' (begin), and an example of the latter type would be 'hotdog' (hot dog). Although it should be noted that there is generally more scope for semantic divergence between the cognate words in the two languages where cognateness is the result of a shared historical etymology, distinguishing between the two types is not important for the practical purposes of the present study for two reasons: a) the synonym choices in the sentences of the gapfilling exercise specifically involve cognates that share a common etymology, and b) this distinction is not presumed to affect the perception of the words as cognates by L2 users.

When discussing cognates, there has traditionally been much focus on *false friends* in language teaching (perhaps because it is a phenomenon that can produce amusing or embarrassing results), but in fact the proportion of "good cognates", i.e. cognates with a wholly or partially shared meaning, is considerably larger than that of "deceptive cognates". Although Granger (1993) is critical of underestimating the proportion of deceptive French cognates in English, she concludes by advocating a balanced approach to cognates in language teaching:

> ...cognates are both an aid and a barrier to successful L2 vocabulary development. Teachers should therefore seek to find a happy medium between over-reliance on cognates and near-pathological mistrust of them, two attitudes which are equally detrimental to learners' vocabulary development. (Granger 1993: 54-55)

Lexical transfer of cognates usually involves both semantic and morphological transfer (Odlin 1989: 82), which could explain why cognates may be particularly attractive candidates for transfer, not least for L2 users who perceive that their L1 is typologically close to English. It would be very surprising if the principle of least possible effort did not apply to language functions as it does to other activities in the natural world in accordance with evolutionary theory. According to Singleton (1999: 152), at the early stages of L2 learning, there is focus on formal aspects of learning a word, whereas the more challenging task of coming to terms with meaning and use follows later. This would appear to make cognates attractive for early L2 learners since most cognates are good cognates and therefore come with the bonus of wholly or partially equivalent meaning.

Also, it has been found that in early stages of L2 learning, the bilingual mind tends to initially map an L2 word form to pre-existing semantic structures of the L1, after which the L2 learner moves on to acquire other L2 words with different semantic content rather than synonyms of already acquired L2 words (Singleton: 1999). When it comes to Danish students of English, the L2 equivalent that is acquired first will often be a Germanic word because such words are more frequent than Latinate words in general and colloquial English where synonyms exist. A number of these Germanic words will be cognates due to the lexical kinship between Danish and English as Germanic languages. For Spanish students, the situation would appear to be reversed, in the sense that they start by perceiving a larger typological distance between the L2 and the L1 at the early stages of L2 learning because the vocabulary of general English language is predominantly Germanic, and Spanish learners will therefore encounter relatively few cognates at the early stages of learning English.

Interestingly, De Groot, Dannenburg, and Van Hell (1994) found that, in the case of cognates, their subjects, first-year university students who had Dutch as their L1 and English as their L2, apparently did not have to resort to conceptual representation in the process of translating. Their response times were faster than for non-cognates, which could indicate that the processing of cognates took place at a formal lexeme level rather than at a conceptual level and that cognates are stored in the bilingual mind in relation to or even as extensions of L1 semantic items, much like inflections and derivations of L1 vocabulary.

Lubliner and Hiebert (2011) investigated why L2 users of English whose L1 is Spanish fail to recognize many of the Spanish cognates in English and found that the challenge is related to orthography. The more difference there is between the forms of the cognate words in the two languages, the harder it is for Spanish L2 English users to identify them as cognates that could provide them with a lexical advantage in learning academic English. Also, a number of Spanish cognates in English are formal in English, whereas the Spanish cognate words are typically everyday words. This is because the vast majority of the most frequently used general words in Spanish are Latinate, unlike English, in which the majority of the most frequent general words are Germanic. However, despite the obstacles posed by typology and psychotypology, Lubliner and Hiebert believe that focused teaching strategies that aim to raise awareness of the 10,000 to 15,000 cognates shared by the Spanish and English languages could be of considerable benefit to L2 English learners whose L1 is Spanish (Lubliner and Hiebert 2011: 77).

Method
For the purpose of testing the hypothesis, approximately 60 Danish university students of L2 English, 60 Spanish university students of L2 English, and 60 American university students whose L1 is English will be enrolled in a gapfilling experiment in which one word has been left out of each of 50 independent sentences. The gapfilling exercise can be found in the appendix, and three sentences are given as examples below:

The two parties to this agreement are the purchaser and the _____.

Over the past three years, the numbers have _____ from 5,484 to 4,608.

The main function of members of a parliament is to pass new _____.

The sentences are constructed so as to provide as much internal semantic context as possible. In each of the sentences, it is possible to insert an English synonym of either Germanic or Latinate origin (*seller* or *vendor*, *fallen* or *decreased*, *laws* or *legislation*).

In one of the other sentences, although there are idiomatic Germanic and Latinate options (*work* or *employment*), it is also possible to insert a word (accompanied by an article) whose etymology cannot be established as either Germanic or Latinate but which is a cognate in Danish (*a job*):

If all else fails, maybe he can find _____ as a dishwasher.

The results for that particular sentence may serve as a test of the presumption that it is cognateness rather than Germanic/Latinate etymology in itself that affects word choice.

In each of the sentences, a Latinate cognate represents an idiomatically precise word choice. This will, it is presumed, increase the significance of the proportion of Germanic words chosen by Danish L2 English users while also exposing the ability of Spanish L2 English users to use English-Spanish cognates. In addition, if Latinate vocabulary is generally a characteristic of high proficiency and if the proficiency of Danish university students of English is generally higher than that of Spanish university students of English, constructing the sentences on the basis of idiomatically precise Latinate choices makes Germanic word choice by the Danish students and Latinate word choice by the Spanish students all the more conspicuous.

When the experiments have been completed, the results of the Danish and Spanish groups will be compared using t-tests[5] to ascertain whether or not the hypothesis may be supported by the results. Also, a one-way ANOVA test[6] will be carried out on the results of the Danish, Spanish, and American groups to test intergroup and intragroup variation for the three groups.

Finally, approximately 60 Danish university students of English will participate in a Danish-language version of the gapfilling experiment in order for the study to meet all three criteria for methodological rigour

---

5   The t-test has one independent variable with only two levels (here: L1 group membership) and one dependent variable (here: the proportion of Germanic words chosen). It asks whether the differences in performance between the two groups are significant enough for them to be attributed to two different populations (Larson-Hall 2010: 136-137).

6   The one-way analysis of variance has one dependent variable (here: the proportion of Germanic words chosen) and one independent variable (here: L1 group membership). The one-way ANOVA compares the variances *within* the groups to the variance *between* the groups to examine whether the differences in performance between the groups are significant enough for them to be attributed to different populations (Larson-Hall 2010: 268).

in identifying evidence of L1 influence in the interlanguage lexicon as proposed by Jarvis (2000): **Intragroup homogeneity** (members of an L1 group of language users perform similarly in the L2), **intergroup heterogeneity** (groups of language users with different L1s perform differently in the L2), and **crosslinguistic performance congruity** (there is congruity between language users' performance in the L1 and their performance in the L2). The third criterion is sometimes not practicable but is always recommended. By conducting a Danish-language version of the gapfilling experiment with Danish university students of L2 English, this study aims to apply all three criteria in the analysis of their performance.

Preliminary results
This study is currently in progress, and only results for 49 Danish university students and 24 American university students are available. Expressed as a percentage, the mean proportion of Germanic English words for the group of Danish students is 48.36%, compared to a mean for the American group of 32.98%. Although the mean for the group of American students is considerably lower than the mean for the group of Danish students, it is too early to draw any conclusions about the hypothesis due to the small size of the American group. It is, however, interesting that the mean for the group of Danish students is relatively high considering that the language providing the internal context in a large number of the sentences is rather formal and that an idiomatically precise Latinate lexical option exists. Also, the preliminary results especially for the Danish students indicate that there may be a link between high proficiency (measured as the ability to insert semantically correct words in the sentences) and a low proportion of Germanic words chosen. This possible relationship will of course be examined in detail when the study has been completed.

Perspectives
After the hypothesis has been tested, the study will proceed to investigate how native English speakers assess the formality of texts containing different proportions of Germanic and Latinate vocabulary.

If Danish university students choose a high proportion of Germanic words in English and if texts containing a high proportion of Germanic words are less formal in the judgment of native English speakers, it would seem reasonable to take this into account when developing English programmes for Danish learners (and possibly also other learners with a Germanic L1) and focus on non-Germanic English vocabulary learning in order to help increase the formality level of learners in academic contexts.

Regarding Spanish L2 English learners, if Spanish university students of English are not as effective in using Latinate cognate words as they could be, considering the large number of English-Spanish cognates, Spanish L2 English learners might benefit from specifically developing their awareness of cognate English vocabulary as a helpful tool, especially in learning English for academic/formal purposes.

Finally, if native English speakers consider the formality of some texts to be inappropriate in terms of linguistic register and their assessment may be related to the proportions of Germanic and Latinate vocabulary in such texts, the study will provide empirical support for the importance of word choice as a component of lexical L2 proficiency.

References

Bar-Ilan, Laly, and Ruth A. Berman. 2007. "Developing register differentiation: The Latinate-Germanic divide in English." *Linguistics: an interdisciplinary journal of the language sciences* 45 (1): 1-36.

Baugh, Albert C., and Thomas Cable. 1993. *A History of the English Language*. New York: Routledge.

Bauman, John, and Brent Culligan. 1995. *About the General Service List*. Accessed May 14, 2013. http://jbauman.com/aboutgsl.html

Coxhead, Averil. 2000. A New Academic Word List. *TESOL Quarterly* 34 (2): 213-238.

Crystal, David. 1997. *Dictionary of Linguistics and Phonetics*. Oxford: Blackwell.

Crystal, David. 1995. *The Cambridge Encyclopedia of the English Language*. Cambridge: Cambridge University Press.

Dagut, Menachem, and Batia Laufer. 1985. "Avoidance of phrasal verbs by Hebrew-speaking learners of English - a case for contrastive analysis."*Studies in Second Language Acquisition*7: 73-79.

De Groot, Annette M. B., Lucia Dannenburg, and Janet G. Van Hell. 1994. "Forward and backward word translation by bilinguals." *Journal of Memory and Language* 33: 600-629.

EF (Education First). 2012. "EPI (English Proficiency Index)". Accessed May 14, 2013.http://www.ef.com/epi/

Granger, Sylviane. 1993."Cognates: an aid or a barrier to successful L2 vocabulary development?" *ITL Review of Applied Linguistics* 99-100: 43-76.

Jarvis, Scott. 2000. "Methodological rigor in the study of transfer: Identifying L1 influence in the interlanguage lexicon." *Language Learning* 50 (2): 245-309.

Jarvis, Scott, and Aneta Pavlenko. 2008. *Crosslinguistic Influence in Language and Cognition*. New York: Routledge.

Kellerman, Eric. 1983. "Now you see it, now you don't." In *Language Transfer in Language Learning*, edited by Susan Gass.and Larry Selinker, 112-134. Rowley, MA: Newbury House.

Larson-Hall, Jenifer. 2010. *A Guide to Doing Statistics in Second Language Research Using SPSS*. New York: Routledge.

Laufer, Batia, and Stig Eliasson. 1993. "What causes avoidance in L2 learning: L1-L2 differences, L1-L2 similarity, or L2 complexity?" *Studies in Second Language Acquisition* 15: 35-48.

Levin, Harry, Howard Giles, and Peter Garrett. 1994. "The Effects of Lexical Formality and Accent on Trait Atrributions." *Language & Communication* 14 (3), 265-274.

Levin, Harry, and Margaretta Novak. 1991. "Frequencies of Latinate and Germanic words in English as determinants of formality." *Discourse Processes* 14 (3), 389-398.

Lubliner, Shira, and Elfrieda H. Hiebert. 2011. "An Analysis of English-Spanish Cognates as a Source of General Academic Language." *Bilingual Research Journal* 34: 76-93.

Odlin, Terence. 1989. *Language Transfer. Cross-linguistic Influence in Language Learning*. Cambridge: Cambridge University Press.

Ringbom, Håkan. 2007. *Cross-linguistic Similarity in Foreign Language Learning*. Clevedon: Multilingual Matters.

Serrander, Ulrika. 2011. "Bilingual Lexical Processing in Single Word Production: Swedish Learners of Spanish and the Effects of L2 Immersion." *Studia Linguistica Upsaliensia* 10. Uppsala: Acta Universitatis Upsaliensis.

Singleton, David. 1999. *Exploring the Second Language Mental Lexicon.* Cambridge: Cambridge University Press.

Smith, Jeremy. 1996. *An Historical Study of English: Function, form and change.* London: Routledge.

West, Michael. 1953. *A General Service List of English Words.* London: Longman.

Appendix

Gapfilling exercise
Fill in the gaps in the following 50 sentences with the word(s) that you find most appropriate. Do not use any aids while completing the exercise. Try your best to avoid leaving any blanks.

1. The two parties to this agreement are the purchaser and the _____.

2. The parent company has set up a number of _____ in various countries.

3. We would like to buy that house, but the monthly _____ that my firm pays me is too low.

4. Over the past three years, the numbers have _____ from 5,484 to 4,608.

5. In order to _____ a visa, you must schedule an interview at the US Embassy.

6. He died at his London _____ in Hart Street, Bloomsbury Square, in February 1819.

7. Adverbs are often _____ from adjectives by adding the suffix -ly.

8. We sent you a letter four weeks ago, but we have still not received any _____ from you.

9. _____, she was reluctant to take the job, but after a while, she enjoyed it very much.

10. The agreement that we made does not take effect yet. It _____ on June 1.

11. According to the Bible, God _____ the world in six days.

12. A complete eclipse of the sun _____ very rarely.

13. In the _____ between the two world wars, there was rapid industrial development.

14. If you multiply your monthly income by 12, you can calculate your _____ income.

15. A number of winemakers in Southern Italy receive agricultural _____ from the EU.

16. We have launched a new marketing campaign to _____ our products.

17. They _____ my employment contract, so I am looking for a new position.

18. The main function of members of a parliament is to pass new _____.

19. Driving while under the influence of alcohol is _____ by law in most countries.

20. Someone must be named in an insurance policy as the _____ in the event of your death.

21. Who will _____ responsibility for the rescue operation?

22. The company is nearly 100 years old. It was _____ in 1915.

23. A red light over the entrance _____ that tickets for the performance are sold out.

24. If all else fails, maybe he can find _____ as a dishwasher.

25. To open the cabinet, _____ the key in the keyhole and turn.

26. Transfers, payments and deposits are examples of _____ carried out by a bank.

27. They tried patiently many times, and _____ they succeeded.

28. Will you be marketing the product to other businesses or directly to _____?

29. The new ramp will _____ the entry of wheelchairs.

30. The Coca-Cola Company is still one of the _____ players in the drinks market.

31. Italian and Irish flags look _____, but the Italian flag is red where the Irish is orange.

32. If you _____ the services of an operator, please press 0.

33. How many countries _____ in the World Cup?

34. Our _____ buy the products from us and sell them to customers in their area.

35. The meeting that was originally scheduled for January has been _____ until March.

36. If delivery is late, the supplier may _____ liability for damages.

37. The unemployment rate has _____ from five to eight per cent in just two years.

38. If there are tasks you cannot perform alone, we will be happy to _____ you.

39. The point of imprisoning people is to deprive them of their _____.

40. We don't have time to dine with them. Our train for London _____ at 5.30.

41. At 15,000 dollars I wish I could buy it, but I doubt there are _____ funds in my account.

42. As soon as I walked into the graveyard, I had a strong _____ that this was dangerous.

43. It can be difficult to _____ the meaning of texts that contain many technical terms.

44. On the basis of the information available, this does _____ to be the best solution.

45. She won 10,000 dollars in the lottery? I have never been so _____ when gambling.

46. These are the first ten numbers in _____ order: 10, 9, 8, 7, 6, 5, 4, 3, 2, 1.

47. He didn't need to wear glasses. The school doctor said he had perfect _____.

48. Crime rates are much lower in rural areas than in _____ areas.

49. I will only be able to buy the house if you are willing to _____ the price.

50. 50 Love, hatred, joy, sorrow and fear are all examples of strong _____.

LSP and sociocultural competences. The teaching of comparative Spanish legal language at a Danish university.

Rita Cancino

Abstract
Traditionally a foreign language is taught as a subject that emphasizes only the language itself, and culture is taught as a different subject as if they were two different phenomena. Generally in Denmark, courses in professional languages or Languages for Specific Purpose (LSP) are being considered as purely professional and not as part of cultural studies. Culture as a concept is not linked with LSP, for instance financial or legal language, even if the latter is probably the most culture-bound professional language there is. In their studies of comparative legal language, Spanish-Danish, students are exposed to major challenges of different types. Students have poor knowledge of the Danish legal system and no knowledge of the Spanish legal system. In the Spanish legal language course, students are introduced to various new universes, i.e. the legal universe and the use of Danish and Spanish legal languages. In this paper I will discuss how courses in comparative legal languages have to explicitly reflect and incorporate cultural differences and intercultural competences. Furthermore, I will give a short description of the complexity of legal language and by means of some examples from Danish and Spanish legal languages, I will illustrate some fundamental problems

when 'translating' culture-bound legal terms from one *legal-linguaculture* into another and finally suggest a different view on this LSP.

Introduction

In a world that is increasingly interdependent, learning foreign languages has become a necessity, and the study of a foreign language helps us to expand our view of the world. It exposes us to modes of thought and viewpoints that are available only in the foreign language, and it fosters our understanding of the interrelation between language and human nature. Learning a language of another country helps us to understand its culture. Unless we understand a culture in its own terms, we cannot be said to have gained access to another culture. Only when we perceive something in the way in which it is expressed and as if it were expressed in our mother tongue, we can be said to have 'understood' the expression. Through studying a foreign language, we face new theories and facts and thus learn to adapt to diversity.

If a person wants to have direct access to art and literature expressed in other languages, that person needs to acquire the knowledge of the languages. Only true knowledge of a language can lead to an exact interpretation of a work of literature written in a foreign language. Original expressions are often changed or lost in translation as:

> Translation is transferring the meaning of a text from one language to another, and such transference has to account for the textual, grammatical and pragmatic meanings of the text to be translated, taking into account that meaning necessitates reference to linguistic and non-linguistic factors embedded within the text (Shiyab and Abdullateef 2001).

So true appreciation of art and literature is possible when accessing it in the original language in which the original culture is embedded.

Traditionally, a foreign language is taught as a subject that emphasizes only the language itself, and culture is taught as a different subject. When we at Aalborg University, at the Department of Language and International Business Communication teach our students Language, Culture and Society as two different subjects we tell them implicitly that language and culture are distinct phenomena and that they have nothing in common. Only in a few cases it is possible to integrate culture in a subject, as for instance when teaching comparative legal language; culture is an inherent part of this subject as the roots of law are deeply anchored in history. Furthermore, there is a tendency to treat the various professional languages as completely culture-free. Financial and Legal languages, for instance are not normally linked up with culture as a concept, even if the latter might be one of the most culture-bound professional languages existing. Legal language draws on both general language and financial language and their cultural metaphors. Furthermore, this professional language is rooted in a legal universe in which law has developed over hundreds of years according to the development of society. In Spain, for instance, legal language is influenced from Roman Law, French Law and Latin, and in Denmark, legal language is influenced by Germanic and Nordic law.

Research studies in the fields of general education and language pedagogy recognize the importance of metaphors both as a research tool and as an important tool in teaching (Kramsch 2003). Nowadays, apart from being a powerful tool of expression and a figure of speech, metaphors are recognized as a "fundamental vehicle of human thought" (Kliebard 1982, 13), an "important tool of cognition and communication" (Ortony & Fainsilber1989, 181) that reflects "images of social phenomenon" (Morgan 1983, 21) through "mapping two often incompatible domains into one another" (Kramsch 2003, 125). Metaphors possess such "invaluable qualities as expressibility, compactness, and vividness" and are "better conceptualized as single ideas than as individual words" (Ortony, 1975; Ortony & Fainsilber 1989, 182). Due to their functions in human cognition, metaphors can serve as "an important instrument of analysis" (Oxford et al.1998, 45) of everyday human practices and experiences, including professional experience.

In this paper, I will discuss why culture cannot, in my view, be separated from language in the teaching of Languages for Specific Purpose, particularly not in the case of legal language, in which culture is inherent.

Legal language represents a professional language in which culture is embedded in a large number of terms, and it is not possible to teach legal language without teaching culture. As a point of departure, my discussion will be based on some examples from my classes of Spanish legal communication at Aalborg University, Denmark. Another purpose of this paper is, through a discussion of the examples of culture-bound legal terms in Danish and Spanish, to contribute to a different view of legal language as an intercultural subject, not only a culture-free Language for Specific Purpose.

Language and culture

> Language is the principal means whereby we conduct our social lives. When it is used in contexts of communication, it is bound up with culture in multiple and complex ways (Kramsch 1998, 3)

As regards language and culture, it is often thought that the reality expressed in spoken words is the very same as the reality perceived in thought. It is assumed that our speech is based on our thoughts, and that perception and expression are frequently perceived to be synonymous. This idea presumes that what is said is dependent on how it is encoded and decoded in our minds. However, many people subscribe to the opposite view, namely that what we perceive is dependent on the spoken word. To the followers of this idea, language controls thought (Badhesha 2002).

The American anthropological linguist, Edward Sapir (1884-1939) and his pupil Benjamin Lee Whorf (1897-1941) are known for the part they have played in the development of this principle. They picked up an already developed notation that different people speak differently because they think differently, and they think differently because their languages offer them different ways of expressing the world around them. Whorf's views on the interdependence of language and thoughts have become known under the name of the Sapir-Whorf hypothesis, or more commonly the Theory of Linguistic Relativity. The Sapir-Whorf hypothesis claims that the structure of the language we habitually use influences the manner in which we think and behave and shapes our view of reality. This has been supported by the findings that there are cultural differences in the semantic associations evoked by seemingly shared concepts, which is generally accepted nowadays. The way in which a given language encodes experience semantically makes aspects of that experience not exclusively accessible, but just more salient for the users of that language (Mooney 2011). The Sapir-Whorf hypothesis is a mould theory "which represents language as a mould in terms of which thought categories are cast" (Chandler 2002, 1).

The Sapir-Whorf theory can be divided into two basic components: Linguistic Determinism and Linguistic Relativism. Linguistic Determinism refers to the concept that what has been said has only some effect on how concepts are recognized by the mind. This basic concept has been broken down even further to "strong" and "weak" determinism (The Sapir-Whorf Hypotheses 2002) and Linguistic Relativity. In 'strong determinism' a person's view of the world is strictly defined by language and what is said is directly responsible for what is seen by the mind. 'Weak determinism' recognizes that language does not define a person's view of the world (Badhesha 2002).

The second component in the Sapir-Whorf Hypothesis is Linguistic Relativism. This part of the hypothesis can be defined as: "distinctions encoded in one language are unique to that language" and "there is no limit to the structural diversity of language" (The Sapir-Whorf Hypothesis 2002, 1). This concept introduces the idea that language is relative, and so a word can mean different things to different people, who each have their own subjective understanding of meaning. According to Sapir:

> Human beings do not live in the objective world alone, nor alone in the world of social activity as ordinarily understood, but are very much at the mercy of the particular language which has become the medium of expression for their society... The fact of the matter is that the "real world" is to a large extent unconsciously built on the language habits of the group... We see and hear and otherwise experience very largely as we

do because the language habits of our community predispose certain choices of interpretation (as cited in Littlejohn 2002, 177).

This view of cognition could provide a more simple definition of meaning: the language in which we are brought up and taught and to which we are socially exposed is the language in which we will think and perceive the world. Furthermore, the language, culture and atmosphere in which we are brought up has an effect on the way in which we decode and encode the meaning of a word, and this cannot always be translated.

The speakers of most languages have adopted a common principle in the conceptualisation of time, for instance. The universal perception is that 'time' must have a backward point and a forward point relative to ourselves. However, some languages construct the future behind and the past in front, as the future is unknown, and what is behind cannot be easily seen, while the past is known, because it has been accomplished (Holme 2003). One such language is the indigenous language Aymará spoken by the Aymará people in Chile. This language has been studied by Núñez and Sweetser (2006) and they describe how the Aymará people perceive time.

One extremely dominant and salient pattern is the ego-RP metaphor Time Is Ego's Motion Along a Path; its experiential basis is clearly universal, and the metaphor itself is so nearly universal that we cannot deny its cognitive accessibility to all humans. Instead of Time Is Ego's Motion Along a Path, Aymará uses a static mapping of past and future onto the space in front of and behind ego, respectively.

This mapping, although its underlying correlations are potentially accessible to any human, has distinctly less elaborate inferential mappings between source and target domains; this may account for its rarity as a primary metaphor of time. Unusual though it may be, gestural as well as linguistic data strongly and systematically attest to its cognitive reality in Aymará speakers. The study of the peculiar Aymará spatial construals of time provides an excellent opportunity to study how fundamental abstract everyday concepts such as time, although ultimately grounded in the same universal human bodily experience of the world, can get shaped in specific ways to generate cultural variability (Nuñez and Sweetser 2006, 42).

"The language transmits a cultural value in its core structure" (Lakoff & Johnson 1999, 141). This example from the Aymará people makes a clear point about the way in which a culture achieves a given effect. This type of examples has caused some cognitive linguists to revisit Whorfian relativism, but with a different conclusion, i.e. that the pattern implicit in the language does not impose itself on a culture's modes of thought; rather, the metaphors through which a culture conceptualises reality impose themselves upon language (Gibbs 1994, 438-45).

According to Kramsch (1998), the words people utter refer to common experience. They express facts, ideas or events in referring to a stock of knowledge about the world. They also express attitudes, beliefs etc. and in both cases, "language expresses cultural reality", and through all its verbal and non-verbal aspects, "language embodies cultural reality" (Kramsch 1998, 3). Language is also a system of signs that are seen as having their own cultural value. Speakers identify themselves and others through their use of language; they view their language as a symbol of their social identity. Thus we may say that language "simbolizes cultural reality" (Kramsch 1998, 3).

One way of thinking of culture is to contrast it with nature. Nature refers to what is born and grows organically; culture refers to what has been grown and groomed (Kramsch 1998). The use of written language is also shaped and socialized through culture. The cultural ways which can be identified at any one time have evolved and become well-established over time, which is why they are so often taken for natural behaviour (Kramsch 1998). "Language is not a culture-free code, distinct from the way people think and behave, but, rather, it plays a major role in the perpetuation of culture, particularly in its printed form" (Kramsch 1998, 8).

Liddicot agrees with Kramsch, stating that language is culture. Language plays a central role in the transmission of cultural codes.

Culture shapes what we say, when we say it, and how we say it from the simplest language we use to the most complex. It is fundamental to the way we speak, write, listen and read. Language has a central role in the transmission of cultural codes; language forms and the messages conveyed by them provide cultural knowledge. Hence the impossibility of separating language and culture (Liddicoat 2002, 5).

Culture in teaching: Different principles and approaches
The Oxford English Dictionary defines 'principle' as a fundamental truth or proposition that serves as the foundation for a system of belief or behavior or for a chain of reasoning. An 'approach' is defined as a way of dealing with a situation or problem. In the following, both concepts are used by the various researchers, apparently without any sharp distinction.

As regards teaching and learning, the introduction of culture into the language curriculum can be based on five principles suggested by Holme (2003, 18-20): The *communicative view* derives from the communicative approach with its stress on giving the student language that can be put to quick use in a specific context. The *classical-curriculum view* in which the interest of languages is secondary to their functions in accessing routes to alien and, to some degree, enlightening modes of thought. The *instrumental* or *culture-free-language view* proceeds from a common concern in respect of the hidden political and cultural agendas of a language. The *deconstructionist view* embraces many quite different strands of thought, i.e. the cultural construction of text, which indicates that the language student may be manipulated by the implicit messages of a text. Further, the Hallidayan concept of language as social semiotics, which perceives the structure of a language as reflecting the communicative needs of a given social context. The *competence view* contends that the knowledge of the culture of a language is considered essential to the full understanding of the nuances of meaning of a language. Knowledge of a culture presupposes a competence which is essential to be able to grasp the true meaning of a language.

Crozet, Liddicoat and Lo Bianco (1999) distinguish between four broad cultural approaches: *The traditional (high culture) approach*: In this approach, cultural competence about a country can be identified by knowledge of an established canon which is often centered in art, music and literature. *Cultural Studies and Area Studies* treat cultural competence as knowledge of a given country (history, geography, institutions). It is possible to obtain this knowledge without having to deal with the language. *Culture as social practice / social norms* identifies cultural competence as acquired knowledge about the likely conduct of members of a particular cultural group, based on known actions or performances. *Intercultural language learning* identifies culture as the lived experiences of individuals. Interaction between people is context sensitive, negotiated, mediated and variable. With regard to learning, it encourages students to develop cultural competence from the moment they start learning a foreign language. None of these cultural approaches can be taught separately. Kramsch (1991) states that culture can be seen as background, indicating the Four F's: foods, fairs, folklore and statistical facts. These four groups correspond to a certain degree with the first two 'views' mentioned by Crozet, Liddicoat and Lo Bianco (1999) and to the first two approaches indicated by Holmes (2003).

As a framework for a discussion of the relations between language and culture in a teaching and learning context, this paper will rely on the cultural approaches introduced by Crozet, Liddicoat and Lo Bianco (1999) and the key concepts of 'Intercultural Language Learning' (abbreviated as IcLL or ILT). Focus will be on the concepts of 'culture' and its place in language learning and 'interculture' as the aim of language learning. Furthermore, 'the third place' will be introduced, a concept which refers to a sort of cultural 'meeting place' in which the understanding of how different worldviews operate makes it possible to move from one language to another.

Framework of Intercultural Language Learning
According to Crozet, Liddicoat and Lo Bianco (1999), in language teaching 'culture' is not the fifth macro-skill (in addition to the skills of speaking, listening, reading and writing) as seen in Damen (1987) – it is integrated

in all skills, and at all levels: even very simple language conveys culture, and it is simply not possible to teach language in a cultural vacuum. So 'culture' is not a separate skill, but an inherent part of language. Crozet, Liddicoat and Lo Bianco point to the fact that even methods of language teaching whose proclaimed aim is to teach people to communicate across cultures have not treated culture as an inherent part of language, Crozet, Liddicoat and Lo Bianco mention both the direct method, the audio-lingual method, and the Communicative Approach, stating that:

> The Communicative Approach as the most current and widely spread approach for language teaching in the Western world today has not significantly improved the teaching of communication in a foreign language. It also has not significantly contributed to the promotion of intercultural competence or cross-cultural understandings (Crozet, Liddicoat and Lo Bianco 1999, 10).

Crozet, Liddicoat and Lo Bianco substantiate this claim by referring to the ways in which language teaching still remains mainly based on written forms; the inseparability of language and culture is still being underplayed: language itself *is* culture, but this understanding of language (and culture) has not been adopted into actual language teaching.

ILT supports the development of the learner's intercultural competence. This is much in line with the current emphasis in language teaching on 'communicative competences', one of which is intercultural competence (Crozet, Liddicoat and Lo Bianco 1999, 12). ILT adopts the notion of *linguaculture* coined by Attinasi and Friedrich in 1988 (Attinasi and Friedrich as cited in Crozet, Liddicoat and Lo Bianco 1999). It is characteristic of ILT that it focuses not only on the target *linguaculture*, but also on the learner's first *linguaculture*. It compares the first language/culture and the target language/culture of learners. Methodologically, this is nothing new as methods of foreign language teaching have always contained an element of comparison. However, ILT's focus on the inseparability of language and culture, *even* in the learner's first *linguaculture*, distinguishes the method from former comparative methods: "... every presentational and comparative language teaching activity is a potentially rich source for foregrounding cultural difference within a framework of similarity" (Crozet, Liddicoat and Lo Bianco 1999, 12).

Through this ILT method learners will develop their intercultural competences. For Crozet, Liddicoat and Lo Bianco, intercultural competence means "the ability to recognise where and when culture is manifest in cross-cultural encounters and the ability to manage an intercultural space where all parties to the encounter are comfortable participants" (Crozet, Liddicoat and Lo Bianco 1999, 13). Consequently, developing intercultural competences through language learning involves acquiring a (better) understanding of the operation of the worldview of the learner's first *linguaculture* and an awareness of a person's cultural boundaries. 'The third space' then refers to a 'meeting place' where the understanding of how different worldviews operate (in one's own *linguaculture* and in foreign *linguacultures*) "frees the mind to explore and at the same time to create interculturality" (Crozet, Liddicoat and Lo Bianco 1999,13).

*Inter*culturality and language teaching
According to Liddicoat, Crozet and Lo Bianco (1999, 181) ILT signifies a move away from the traditional conception of language proficiency. In ILT, the aim of turning the learner into an almost native speaker is replaced by an aim of making him or her comfortable and capable in an intercultural context. "The native speaker norm is replaced by a bilingual norm as the desirable outcome of language teaching and learning"(Liddicoat, Crozet and Lo Bianco 1999, 181). Consequently, the language learner is not viewed as a "defective native speaker" but as "'a user of language drawing upon the resources available to him/her" (Liddicoat, Crozet and Lo Bianco 1999, 181 – emphasis original). This intercultural context is characterized by a need for language users to use multiple perspectives to understand and create meaning. Language users are *inter*cultural language users when inhabiting 'the third place', as defined by Liddicoat, Crozet and Lo Bianco:

> The third space can only be established as a validation of both self and other. Both the original and the evolving cultural identity of the learner need to be valued and included explicit-

ly in the process. Also the target culture needs to be valued and included. The process is not one of competition between each pole, with one inevitably replacing the other, rather it is a continual negotiation between the poles, until learners find a comfortable position leading to a hybrid third place for themselves (Liddicoat, Crozet and Lo Bianco 1999, 182).

Thus, language learners should not strive for assimilation into the target language, but instead work towards establishing a 'third place' in which several *linguacultures* are negotiated. ICL also calls for the reconceptualization of 'language'. Language is seen as something beyond the linguistic code, and it is therefore not enough for language learners to gain knowledge of grammar, pronunciation and vocabulary. And it is not a question of simply 'adding' new modules to the code (e.g. pragmatics and discourse); it is a question of recognizing that "the linguistic code itself is situated practice as well as an artefact" (Liddicoat, Crozet and Lo Bianco 1999, 182). This also means that "culture cannot be an added module" but must be recognized, also in practice, as inseparable from the code. "Culture is also variable and interactional. It is created by talk and creates talk" (Liddicoat, Crozet and Lo Bianco 1999, 183). Furthermore, Liddicoat argues in favour of a "dynamic approach" to culture "which views culture as sets of variable practices in which people engage in order to live their lives, and which are continually created and recreated by participants in interaction" (Liddicoat 2004, 301). On the basis of this understanding of culture as *variable practices*, Liddicoat concludes that cultural knowledge is not about learning about a culture (its facts and artefacts) but about how to engage with that culture (through language). Consequently,"the scope of culture learning moves beyond awareness, understanding and sympathy and begins to address the ways in which culture learning will be practised by learners" (Liddicoat 2004, 301). But as Liddicoat has pointed out, a gap sometimes exits between proclaimed aims and actual teaching, which means that designers of language courses must be much aware of how to put into practice the idea of integrated language and culture teaching, and how to ensure that the language teaching will actually make learners develop their intercultural competences.

Teaching/learning comparative legal language Spanish-Danish

> Such learners need to function fully in a situation where at least two languages and two cultures, their own and another one, interplay and they may find themselves in a no-man's land or, more exactly, in a "third place" from which they must understand and mediate between the home and the target language and culture (Kramsch 1993, 233-259).

In the remaining part of this paper I will discuss some of the challenges faced in the teaching of comparative Spanish legal language at a Danish university. In the following discussion of the challenges which apply to this particular discipline, I will explain how the approach to language and culture can be put into practice. As mentioned previously, ILT focuses not only on the target *linguaculture*, but also on the learner's first *linguaculture*. As the focus area is legal language in Denmark and Spain together with the embedded culture, I will extend the concept *linguaculture* to the legal world by introducing a new concept into the discussion which I will name *legal-linguaculture*.

The teaching and learning of comparative legal language Spanish-Danish covers various serious challenges, as with its many Latin terms, Spanish law is rooted in ancient Roman law, whereas Danish Law has its roots in Germanic and Nordic Law. The problem is not that language embeds culture, but that legal language embeds ancient (legal) culture in both Danish and Spanish legal languages and introduces the students to hitherto unknown and complex concepts. Furthermore, our own culture is often hardly visible to us as since childhood we have been exposed to a national culture which to us represents 'normality'. Danish students do not see their own culture until confronted with a culture which is completely different. Maria José Aguilar gives a possible explanation to this 'blindness' to one's own culture:

> We are so familiar to our own culture that we don't even realize it is there and, inevitably, it influences our expectations when we establish contact with people belonging to a different culture. [...] Driven by ethnocentrism, we tend to take as 'normal'

> what we know, what we are familiar with, and when confronted
> with new situations we may lose footing. (Aguilar 2008, 62)

According to Lakoff & Johnson (1980), languages are built around conceptualisations in the shape of conceptual metaphors. These metaphors play a considerable role in the construction of language by culture and in the transmission of culture as language. In this way, languages transmit the modes of thought that have evolved in ancient and lost cultures. In their capacity of colonial powers, languages such as Latin, Spanish and English may carry their inherited modes of thought across to their colonies while bending to new expressive needs, remodeling the metaphors they inherit or changing them in new ways.

During history, several of the present European countries and nations were exposed to conquests and immigration from many different peoples. Once, England was also conquered by several peoples, for instance the Romans; as a consequence, English Law draws upon a legal framework that is one of the legacies of the ancient Roman civilization, whose language was the classical Latin language. Wherever the Romans conquered or exerted their influence, their culture was gradually extended to and accepted by the local people. Two enduring heritages have been the impact of Latin on the native languages of the conquered areas, and the influence of Roman law on the subsequent legal system (Tiersma 1999). In Denmark, Canonical Law played an important role in the development of Danish Law in the Middle Ages. Many Latin terms and expressions were introduced by this Canonic Law from the Roman-Catholic Church, and still many Latin expressions remain in Danish legal language. Spanish legal language contains a considerable number of metaphors, according to Cuadrado (2003, 74). In the past, many Spanish words and expressions were metaphors, but later they passed onto the legal language without being considered as such. Still, many of them can be identified, and therefore several conceptual metaphors exist in current Spanish legal language. An example is the expression *cadena perpetua* which literally means 'unceasing chain', but it is the Spanish legal term for 'life imprisonment'. Spanish legal metaphors have also invaded common language as it is possible to say *Ha hipotecado su porvenir con ese trabajo que ha aceptado*, which means that a person is exposing his future to danger because of his new job. *Hipotecar* as a legal term means to 'pledge' something.

The above-mentioned factors indicate that when learning comparative legal language, Spanish-Danish students are exposed to severe challenges of different kinds. The BA-students start a new academic discipline with a considerable amount of culture-bound content at their third semester. They do not know much about Danish Law, the Danish legal system or Danish legal language. Concerning Spanish legal language, Spanish Law and the Spanish legal system, the same conditions are applicable, as students do not have any knowledge of this field. Furthermore, students' competencies in Spanish are scarce after only two semesters of Spanish studies at university. When starting the course of Spanish legal communication, students are introduced to various new universes, i.e. the legal world and the legal languages used in Denmark and Spain. In nine weeks, with two lessons every week, with exercises in the shape of translations from Danish to Spanish and vice-versa, students are expected to able to pass an exam documenting their knowledge of both the legal systems and the legal languages in the two countries. This constitutes a challenge to both students and teacher. Evidently, the problems arise particularly in connection with Spanish and Danish legal terms which have no equivalent terms in the other language because of the cultural (historical) differences between the two legal systems and the two countries. In the following sections, some examples will be given of the degree of complexity which exists in connection with the translation of the Spanish legal terms.

How to translate Juez de Paz?
One of the recurring problems for the students is the court system in Spain compared to the Danish system. In Spain, there is, for instance, a judge called Juez de Paz (Judge of the Peace) placed at los Juzgados de Paz (The Justice of the Peace). This judge sits in small communities with no First Instance and Instruction Courts. They hear minor civil cases, among their functions, and they sometimes work as a Civil Registry Body. The Provincial Court appoints these Judges for a period of four years. Furthermore, the Juez de Paz has no legal degree from a university.

According to Crozet, Liddicoat and Lo Bianco (1999), it is necessary for the students to explore 'the first place' in order to see and understand how the situation is dealt with in their own language. They have to learn how the first *linguaculture* operates and to achieve awareness of their own cultural boundaries. Subsequently they move to 'the second place', which means that they need to understand how the situation is dealt with in the target language and the target culture. Here they must reflect on the similarities and differences between first and second places. Finally, they arrive at 'the third place', a meeting place in which each student reaches a response to the situation and where "the understanding of how different worldviews operate (in their own *linguaculture* and in foreign *linguacultures*) frees the mind to explore and at the same time to create interculturality" (Crozet, Liddicoat and Lo Bianco 1999, 13).

Following Crozet, Liddicoat and Lo Bianco's ideas, the students will need to familiarize themselves with 'the first place', which is the Danish Courts System. In Denmark a judge can sit in the District Court, the High Court and the Supreme Court, according to the general system. In order for them to acquire an overview of the Danish system, the students are then introduced in class to a chart showing the Danish Court Hierarchy; the lowest step in this is the District Court.

After this introduction, the students are ready to move on to 'the second place', which means that they need to become accustomed to the Spanish Court System; this is much more complicated than the Danish system due to the number of instances. The Justice of the Peace in Spain originates in the Civil Procedure Act 1855 and the Decree of 22 October the same year. The Justice of the Peace (*Juzgados de Paz*) is the lowest step in the Spanish Court System. Here the students are also given an overview of the legal system in Spain in the form of a chart showing the position of the Juez de Paz in the hierarchy. Following this, it should be possible to reach 'the third place' with the introduction of a new concept into Danish legal language, a concept which does not exist in Denmark and in the Danish Court System. This new concept is the term *Fredsdommer* (which is the literal translation of Juez de Paz). This concept does not exist in the Danish Court Hierarchy and in Danish *legal-linguaculture*, but the students have now reached a point where they can handle this new concept.

***Spanish DNI versus Danish CPR-number/Sundhedsbevis* (Healths Insurance Card).**

Identity documentation is an important means for defining the members of a nation. Significant differences exist between the embedded cultural aspects of the Spanish and Danish *legal-linguacultures*, respectively. All Spaniards are entitled to a DNI, *Documento Nacional de Identidad*, national identity card, and this is mandatory for everyone over 14 years living in Spain. The DNI dates to the times of the deceased Spanish dictator, General Franco, and the first card was issued in 1944 as a result of the chaos left by the Spanish Civil War with many citizens missing. The DNI is a plastic card issued by the Spanish Home Ministry which includes a photo, a signature and a microchip with personal information and the Spanish text in all the four Spanish national languages. Every Spanish citizen must present their DNI on request in order to identify themselves, and the DNI constitutes sufficient identity documentation when travelling in the EU and many other countries. The DNI Electronic is replacing the traditional DNI and more new applications are received for this. Once more the students must move to the 'first place', their native *legal-linguaculture*. Denmark does not have any official identity card equivalent to the Spanish DNI. The closest we get to the DNI in a Danish context is the Danish *sundhedsbevis* (Health Insurance Certificate), a plastic card showing a *CPR-nummer* (Personal Identification Number) which includes a person's date and year of birth plus four additional digits. All Danish Personal Identification numbers are kept in a central register managed by the Danish State. The current Danish national health insurance system dates back to 1971, and it ensures all Danish citizens free medical treatment. The certificate is issued by the local authorities to all citizens (including all children), and the card must be presented at the doctor's and in hospitals. The *sundhedsbevis* is becoming increasingly important as the amount of data in the chip is increasing.

Moving to 'the second place', the students have to become accustomed to the Spanish identification system and to the very important role played by the DNI in Spain. On their way to 'the third place' the students have to learn that the DNI satisfies other needs and cannot be compared to the Danish *sundhedsbevis*. The latter is not an official ID card as it does not contain a photo, and it cannot be used in the same official situations as the Spanish DNI. For identification, Danish citizens can use their driver's licence as it contains a photo of its owner, but since not all citizens have a driver's licence, this does not correspond to the DNI either. Finally, the most official Danish identification document (with both photo and signature) is the passport, but it is not required of Danish citizens that they have a passport unless they want to travel outside the Schengen-countries. Consequently, Denmark does not have an equivalent to the Spanish DNI. However, the *sundhedsbevis* is the closest we get to a national identity card as all Danish citizens hold this card. When reaching 'the third place', the students have achieved new knowledge about their own and the Spanish *legal-linguacultures,* and they have met a new concept, the *legitimationskort,* which is the Danish interpretation of the Spanish DNI, a concept which does not exist in Danish legal language.

The intercultural context, in this case the Spanish, is characterized by a need for language users to use multiple perspectives to understand and create meaning. Language users are *inter*cultural language users when they inhabit 'the third place', as Liddicoat, Crozet and Lo Bianco define this:

> The third space can only be established as a validation of both self and other. Both the original and the evolving cultural identity of the learner need to be valued and included explicitly in the process. Also the target culture needs to be valued and included. The process is not one of competition between each pole, with one inevitably replacing the other, rather it is a continual negotiation between the poles, until learners find a comfortable position leading to a hybrid third place for themselves (Liddicoat, Crozet and Lo Bianco 1999, 182).

On the basis of this understanding of culture as *variable practices*, Liddicoat concludes that cultural knowledge is not acquired by learning about a culture (its facts and artefacts), but by learning to engage with that culture (through language) (Liddicoat 2004, 301). The above-mentioned examples show clearly that teaching a Language for Specific Purpose, in this case Legal Language, is also the teaching of culture and, for that matter, of knowledge of society. The students can achieve many intercultural skills through these courses in which they are inevitably confronted with not only culture belonging to the field of law but also to culture in general. Here, culture is embedded in the legal terms, the legal collocations, the judicial hierarchy, in linguistic terms, in real terms and phrases, in legal stereotypes etc. By learning legal language the students also achieve intercultural competences, but they are not aware of this because the concept of culture almost always remains an isolated subject and is not normally seen to be related to a professional language.

Conclusion
The Sapir-Whorf hypothesis, which conveys Whorf's views on the interdependence of language and thoughts, elaborated on an already developed perception that different people speak differently because they think differently. The reason why they think differently is that their languages offer them different ways of expressing the world around them. This hypothesis makes the claim that the structure of the language habitually used influences the manner in which we think and behave. Today it is widely accepted that cultural differences appear in the semantic associations of seemingly common concepts.

Students who are languages learners should be able to interact with people, to negotiate meaning and to establish interpersonal relations across languages and cultures. The process of acquiring a language is understood as an unconscious process in which language students develop hypotheses about languages based on the meaningful inputs they receive. The acquisition occurs when a language student understands a message in the new language. This means that learning a language is rather a conscious process which includes memory, understanding and thoughts about the language in question. When learning comparative legal language Spanish-Danish, the students, who were generally brought up in a Danish culture and see the world from a Danish perspective, are exposed to severe challenges of different kinds. Generally, students have insignificant knowledge of Danish law, the Danish legal system and the Danish legal language. Knowledge of the Spanish legal language, Spanish law and the Spanish legal system is non-existing. The Spanish Legal Language course introduces students to a new world in which they must achieve knowledge of how legal language is used in Denmark and Spain.

Courses in comparative legal languages must reflect and incorporate cultural differences and intercultural competences even at beginner's level. Students need to understand legal terms from two different worlds and to know how to combine them in the so-called 'third place', which means overcoming the typical blindness to one's own culture. The examples used in the paper illustrate some fundamental problems when 'translating' words from one *legal-linguaculture* into another.

Furthermore, cognitive metaphors and a common glossary are not adequate to ensure the comparability and consistency among courses in different languages and different *legal-linguacultures*: Culture cannot and should not be isolated as a subject, as culture is embedded in all types of language. Legal language, a LSP, is also cultural training in which the students achieve intercultural competences as culture is implicitly present in the legal terms, fixed expressions, metaphors, collocations, etc. in the shape of historical, societal and legal knowledge. In the future, the legal language course should be renamed 'Legal Language & Legal Intercultural Skills' in order to arouse students' awareness of the intercultural competences they achieve.

References

Aguilar, María. J. C. 2008. "Dealing with Intercultural Communicative Competence in the Foreign Language Classroom". In *Intercultural Language Use and Language Learning* edited by *Eva Alcón* Soler and María Pilar Safont Jordà, 59-78. Springer.

Badhesha, R. S. 2002. *Sapir-Whorf Hypothesis*. http://zimmer.csufresno.edu/~johnca/spch100/4-9-sapir.htm. Accessed on 15th January 2014.

Chandler, Daniel. 2002. *The Sapir-Whorf Hypothesis*. http://www.aber.ac.uk/media/Documents/short/whorf/html (2002, March). Accessed on 20th January 2013.

Crozet, Chantal, Liddicoat, Anthony and Lo Bianco, Joseph. 1999. "Striving for the Third Place: Intercultural Competence through Language Education" in *Striving for the Third Place: Intercultural Competence through Language Education* edited by Chantal Crozet, Anthony Liddicoat and Joseph Lo Bianco, 181-190. Melbourne: Language Australia.

Cuadrado, Luis Alberto Hernando. 2003. *El lenguaje jurídico.* Madrid: Editorial Verbum S.L. Madrid.

Damen, Louise. 1987. *Culture Learning: the Fifth Dimension in the Language Classroom.* Reading: MA: Addison-Wesley.

Gibbs, Raymond. 1994. *The Poetics of Mind.* Cambridge: Cambridge University Press.

Holme, Randal. 2003. "Carrying a Baby *in* the Back: Teaching with an Awareness of the Cultural Construction of Language"; in *Context and Culture in Language Teaching and Culture* edited by Michael Byram and Peter Grundy. Clevedon. Buffalo. Toronto. Sydney: Multilingual Matters Ltd.

Kliebard, H. M. 1982. "Curriculum theory as metaphor", in: *Theory into practice* 21 (1), 11-17

Kramsch, Claire. 1991. "Culture in Language Learning: A view from the US". In *Foreign Research in Cross Cultural Perspective* edited by Kees de Bot, Ralph G. Ginberg and Claire Kramsch. Amsterdam: John Benjamins.

Kramsch, Claire. 1993. *Context and culture in Language Teaching*. Oxford: University Press. Kramsch, Claire. 1995. "The cultural component of language teaching". In *Language, Culture and Curriculum*, 8(12), 1995, 83-92. http://www.collectionscanada.gc.ca/eppp-archive/100/201/300/zeitschrift/2002/02-05/archive/kramsch2.htm. Accessed on 18th May 2013.

Kramsch, Claire. 1998. *Language and Culture*. Oxford: University Press.

Kramsch, Claire. 2003. *Language Acquisition and Language Socialization: Ecological Perspectives (Advances in Applied Linguistics)*.London, New York: Continuum

Lakoff, George and Johnson, Mark. 1999. *Philosophy in the Flesh*. New York: Basic Books.

Lakoff, George and Johnson, Mark. 1980. *Metaphors we live by*. London and Chicago: University of Chicago Press.

Liddicoat, Anthony, Crozet, Chantal and Lo Bianco, Joseph. 1999. "Striving for the Third Place: Intercultural Competence through Language Education" in *Striving for the Third Place: Intercultural Competence through Language Education* edited by Chantal Crozet, Anthony Liddicoat and Joseph Lo Bianco, 181-190. Melbourne: Language Australia.

Liddicoat, Anthony J. 2002."Static and dynamic views of culture and intercultural language acquisition". *Babel* 36 (3): 4-11, 37.

Liddicoat, Anthony J. 2004."The Conceptualisation of the Cultural Component of Language Teaching in Australian Language-in-education Policy". *Journal of Multilingual and Multicultural Development*, 25 (4): 297-317.

Littlejohn, Stephen. W. 2002. *Theories of Human Communication*. Wadsworth: New Mexico.

Lo Bianco, Joseph. 1999. "Syntax of Peace"? in *Striving for the Third Place: Intercultural Competence through Language Education* edited by Chantal Crozet, Anthony J. Liddicoat and Joseph Lo Bianco, 51-64. Melbourne: Language Australia.

Mooney, Annabelle. 2011. "Language thought and representation". *Language, Society and Power. An introduction*. London and New York: Routledge.

Morgan, Gareth. 1983. "Research strategies: Modes of engagements" in *Beyond method: Strategies for social research*, edited by Gareth Morgan, 19-44. Beverly Hills: Sage.

Ortony, Andrew. 1975:"Why metaphors are necessary and not just nice", in: *Educational Theory* 25: 45-53.

Ortony, Andrew/Fainsilber, Lynn. 1989. "The role of metaphors in descriptions of emotions", in: *Theoretical issues in natural language processing* edited by Yorick Wilks,181-184. Hillsdale, NJ: Erlbaum

Oxford, Rebecca/Tomlinson, Stephen/ Barcelos, Ana/Harrington, Cassandra/Lavine, Roberta Z./ Saleh,Amany/ Longhini, Ana (1998). "Clashing metaphors about classroom teachers: Toward a systematic typology for the language teaching field". *System* 26 (1): 3-50.Pergamon.

Núñez, Rafael E./ Sweetser, Eve. 2006. "With the Future Behind Them: Convergent Evidence From Aymara Language and Gesture in the Crosslinguistic Comparison of Spatial Construals of Time". In *Cognitive Science 30*: 1–49.

Shiyab, Said/ Abdullateef, Mohammad.2001. "Translation and Foreign Language"

Lang. & Trans.! Vol. 13: 1- 9. (A H. 1421/2001). Riyadh, Saudi Arabia.

The Sapir-Whorf Hypotheses. 2002. http.//www.venus.va.com.au/suggestion/sapir.html.

Tiersma, Peter M. 1999. *Legal Language.* The University of Chicago Press: Chicago.

Text competence – a challenge in German legal contracts

Aase Voldgaard Larsen

Abstract
The theme of this paper is text competence, i.e. linguistic and non-linguistic competence, in German tenancy contracts in which one of the parties is a layperson. The lacking text competence of the layperson in the legal area constitutes a challenge in the realm of contracts. The required linguistic knowledge on the lexical and syntactic levels constitutes a problem, and yet another problem is for the layperson to understand the implications of the written text. In this paper, I look into the forms of text competence which are necessary in order for the layperson to understand the contract through a discussion of situational and functional factors.

As it is, the wording in contracts does – to a large extend – draw on non-linguistic knowledge through explicit or implicit references to e.g. the law, judicial decisions and legal literature, which must be inferred by the reader in order to understand the contract text correctly. Two surveys among German lawyers mentioned in this paper show that when formulating the text, the text producers decide whether they want to emphasise the party perspective and thus the action-directing function, or prefer to focus on the court perspective and the control-directing function. Depending on which strategy they choose, their focus is to a smaller or larger degree on the contract comprehensibility for the layperson. In this paper, I investigate which, primarily, linguistic strategies are utilized by text producers to meet the lacking text competences of the layperson, by analysing the two surveys among German lawyers. Finally, I examine if the strategies mentioned by the lawyers can be found again in the wording of a 'layperson-friendly' contract.

Introduction
The system of the law is closely connected to the language of the law. It is impossible to imagine a system of law without a language of law. All events concerning rights and obligations between two parties in contract law, in the legal system (e.g. in court), and in all other legal areas depend on the parties or their representatives sharing a common language for expressing the rights and obligations as well as the argumentation for their stance. Mastering the language of the law is, therefore, an essential requirement for working in the legal universe and is seen by many lawyers and jurists as a matter of immense importance. But using and understanding legal language can constitute a huge challenge for many lay people. The knowledge base that is necessary for understanding the contracts and that is to be activated through inference (Busse 1992) can be divided into "non-linguistic knowledge" (knowledge about the world and situation/context) and "linguistic knowledge" (knowledge about the language used in a given genre in a given situation to express a particular proposition) (Dam and Engberg 2005, 2).

The purpose of this paper is to explore text competence in legal texts, more precisely the types of text competence which need to be exercised in German tenancy contracts in order to ensure that the parties to a contract understand the text, and the strategies which are used in the production process to meet lacking text competences. Text competence must be present with the parties, and the text producer must be aware of the challenge he is facing when he is to produce a contract text. A special problem is involved when one of the parties is a layperson, i.e. a person who has no special insight into the subject of the contract, into the language of contracts and into the situation and function of the contract text – but who only needs to rent a flat to have a place to live. For such situations, it is sometimes found that the text producers use different strategies when producing the text, making adjustments and changes of the contract text in order to take the lacking knowledge and text competence of the layperson into consideration in advance. Thus, the research question posed in this paper is: Which strategies do text producers utilize to meet the lack of text competences of the layperson?

The structure of the paper is as follows: First, the research question and the methodological point of departure as well as the analysis design and the empirical material are set out. A discussion of the forms of text competence necessary for the layperson in order to understand the contract is carried out, forming the basis for the analysis leading to answering the research question. In connection with this discussion, an account of the complexity of the communication situation is given, and the prioritising of the possible functions is described. Then two surveys among German lawyers concerning their strategies in their actual practices when producing contract texts are presented, as well as the reasons they give for changing the wording or not changing the wording of the text in accordance with the nature of the parties. These strategies are compared and related to the wording of a layperson-oriented contract text, focusing on showing if examples of the use of the strategies mentioned can be found in the contract text. The fundamental base of the contract analysis is a collection of analysis instruments that was set out in an analysis model in Larsen (2009). The analysis model is divided into three parts; the lexical level (investigating e.g. terminology, formal lexis and abstract lexis), the syntactic level (investigating e.g. insertions and complexity in sentence structure) and a third level of text references (investigating e.g. explicit and implicit references to other texts), which has been seen to play an important part in legal texts. Finally, the fundamental dilemma of the text producer is discussed.

Genre theory as a frame for analysis
Basically, focus in this paper is on actual language in use. Thus, a usage-oriented view on language in professional communication is pre-

sented. The point of departure of this paper is genre theory. A genre can be defined as a group of texts used in approximately the same types of situations with approximately the same purpose, and constructed with the use of approximately the same linguistic means (Lux 1981). This can be visualized by a triangle model consisting of: Situation, Function and Linguistic means; these three elements are constitutive of a genre. This model was developed in Engberg (1993) and refined and improved in Engberg (1998). [1]

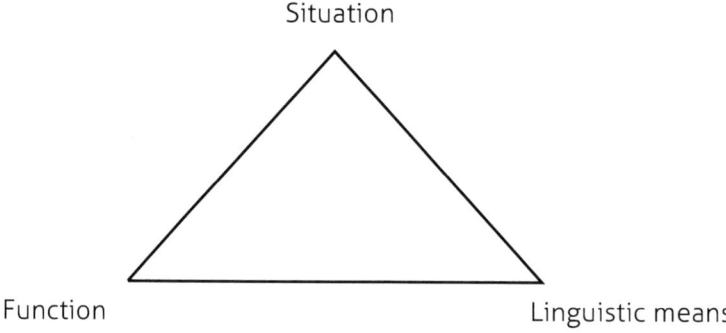

Figure 1: Triangle model of a genre (translated version of the model in Engberg, 1998, 54)

Between Situation and Function is a relation of determination, which means that in some cases situation determines function, and in other cases function determines situation. The relation between Function and Linguistic means is a relation of purpose-and-means, as the linguistic means must be of a certain semantic quality in order to achieve a particular function and a certain function can be fulfilled by particular

---

[1] The model has been modified in the element of Linguistic means by Ditlevsen et al. (2007, 100), thus adding the visual means to the Linguistic means, in order to take into account the importance of visual elements in some genres. Visual elements are, however, less important in legal texts, as there are for example no photos, videos, animations etc. in most legal texts. The visual aspects concerning the writing of the text, e.g. font and pitch size, are not in focus in this paper, therefore the original model will be used here.

linguistic means. The relation between Situation and Linguistic Means can be described as a relation of typicality in which the situation decides on the basis of tradition which linguistic means (that could potentially fulfil the function) are most frequently used, and which become conventionalized (Ditlevsen et al. 2007, 107-109). A text of a specific genre is seen as an individual text adjusted to the situation in which it is applied, and to the function(s) it is supposed to fulfil.

The Situation consists of the actual communication situation and the cultural surroundings, in which the text must function. A text is never simply a text on its own; "it is always embedded in a context and interpreted as representing a conventionalized pattern of communication, a genre" (Kvam, Knutsen and Langemeyer 2010, 32). The context gives meaning to the text (Kvam, Knutsen and Langemeyer 2010, 25).

Contracts are regarded as a genre, and the most important contextual factors of the contract as a genre, especially the communication situation which is rather complex (including different senders and receivers) as well as theme, time, place and medium, are described in this paper. The Function is the purpose or the aim of the text from the sender's point of view in a particular communication situation. This element is determined by the use of the division of functions on the basis of a party perspective and a court perspective (Gunnarsson 1982, 2009), which implies that the text may serve different functions. In this paper, however, the Linguistic means are in focus, and therefore a linguistic analysis focussing on the features at the lexical level, the syntactic level and at reference level, is provided. Legal texts, such as contracts, are conventionally characterized by certain patterns, e.g. extensive use of legal terminology, nominal style and complex sentence structure (cf. Larsen 2009, 121-126), but this study investigates whether differences from these conventional patterns can be seen according to the perspective chosen by the text producer.

The starting point of this part of the analysis is formed by two small, not-representative surveys among German lawyers.[2] The theme of these

---

2   A thorough presentation of the construction of the first survey can be found in Larsen (2009), for which the first survey was carried out, and of the second survey in Larsen (2013).

surveys is the actual practice of the lawyers concerning the formulation of legal agreements, and the question posed was if, in some cases, the lawyers formulate contract texts differently when one of the parties is a layperson, i.e. a consumer, or if they exclusively take other aspects into consideration.[3] The first survey was carried out in 1998-1999 per email among 100 lawyers, of which 51 answered the question. The second survey in 2012 was also conducted per email among the remaining 43 of the 51 responding lawyers from the first survey: a similar question was asked in order to discover any temporal differences. In the new survey, 18 lawyers answered the question. Only a few minor differences between the two surveys were in fact found, and therefore they are treated together in this paper.

In their answers, the lawyers mention several strategies they use in order to ensure that the layperson understands the wording of the contract, and these answers form the basis of a comparison with actual contract texts for the purpose of investigating if the strategies mentioned by the lawyers can be rediscovered in a 'layperson-friendly' contract text.

Two standard tenancy agreements in which one of the parties is a layperson (i.e. the tenant is a consumer) were analyzed. Standard agreements are contract forms, typically retrieved or bought from the internet, for example from a tenants' association or a landlords' association, or bought in a physical paper shop. They were formulated by the text producer in a way that renders them directly useable in actual situations. The form only needs to be completed by filling in names, addresses and numbers as well as crosses in boxes, and if desired also by adding terms and conditions in a concluding section entitled for instance "Additional terms" (in German e.g. "Sonstige Vereinbarungen"). Standard contracts were chosen because they are particularly capable of influencing the world as they are used by many people directly or taken as a source of inspiration for the production of other texts. The purpose of this study is not to see how they can be rephrased by lawyers in actual situations, but to examine how different standard tenancy contracts were formulated originally.

---

3   The actually asked question in the second survey was slightly moderated compared to the question in the first survey due to some unfortunate presuppositions of the first question (cf. Larsen 2009, 2013).

One of the contracts is a layperson-oriented contract (Deutscher Mieterbund 2013) which is seen to have been modified in a number of areas in order to accommodate the layperson, and the other is a conventional agreement (Grundeigentum-Verlag 2013) which is characterized by linguistic means conventional in legal contracts. The conventional text will not be referred to directly, but has been used as a basis of comparison in the preparatory work for this paper. These two contracts are written texts, made available on the internet for download and printing without or with payment respectively, and they were made for application in real tenancy relationships in Germany in 2013.

Text competence: Linguistic and non-linguistic competence
A wide range of competences are necessary for producing and understanding a text, for example a legal contract. But it can be difficult to distinguish between linguistic competence or knowledge on the one hand and non-linguistic competence or knowledge on the other hand. Although, for various research reasons, distinctions are made between these competences (Dam and Engberg 2005, 2), it is important to say that one cannot be seen without the other in the field of text linguistics in the legal universe, as they are closely interwoven. "How we relate to texts depends on our text competence" (Kvam, Knutsen and Langemeyer 2010, 25). Therefore, the concept "text competence" is chosen for this paper to comprise both linguistic and non-linguistic competences.

The term "knowledge" is also important when taking a step backwards and pointing out the origin of the competences in question. Linguistic and non-linguistic competences are based on knowledge, as knowledge is necessary, according to Busse (2004): textual formulas can only be filled with meaning on the basis of a certain knowledge base (Busse 2004, 10). A cognitive act of inference is performed when filling a textual formula with meaning, and the presupposed knowledge base necessary for the inference forms an immense problem for many laypeople. A layperson is seen by the lawmakers as deficient in his knowledge base (BGB 2003, XXVIII) and in his competence of inferring the knowledge he might have. In fact, the introduction to the central civil law in Germany, Bürgerliches Gesetzbuch, states that the layperson, in this case the consumer, needs protection and might risk unfair treatment, because of the economic or intellectual superiority of his contract partner (BGB 2003, XXVIII). This is not true of all laypeople, of course; some of them are very well informed and this could be called expert laity (Sarangi 2001). Nevertheless it is true of many laypeople.

The layperson is lacking in linguistic knowledge, i.e. "knowledge about the language we use" (Dam and Engberg 2005, 2), which means the language typically used in the particular genre in the particular situation in order to realize a function through a particular utterance (cf. the genre definition above). This might be legal or economic terms, the specific syntactic varieties used in legal contracts, as well as other kinds of wording and its precise implications, which are based on phrases, terms and conditions in the law, in previous judicial decisions and in juridical literature. Thus, linguistic knowledge cannot be seen as isolated in legal texts, due to the fact that language is so closely connected to an underlying non-linguistic system. The layperson only possesses a limited amount of knowledge of this system, i.e. the terms and conditions and the traditions in the legal field in question (Busse 1992). This means that the layperson is lacking non-linguistic knowledge of the situation and "knowledge of the world we talk about" [4] (Dam and Engberg 2005, 2).

Due to the lacking knowledge and text competence, the layperson – as a communication party – finds himself in a weaker position than the other party of the communication (White 1982, 422; Iversen et al. 1992, 112; Larsen 2009). To put it simple, he just needs new accommodation and must therefore enter into a contract. He is not normally occupied with texts of this type, and he therefore has only limited knowledge of the law and the genre, and he might not be able to foresee or take an overall view of the legal implications of the different possibilities of wording.

---

4   In this paper it is not particularly important to distinguish between "world/encyclopaedic/background knowledge" and "situational/contextual knowledge". Therefore, world and situational knowledge are referred to as non-linguistic knowledge (Dam and Engberg 2005, 2).

Therefore he might experience excessive disadvantage, because the landlord can be seen as his superior intellectually and financially (Bürgerliches Gesetzbuch 2003, XXVIII).

It might be worth discussing if the other party to the contract, the landlord, is in fact also a layperson, a semi-expert or an expert. However, this is not the topic of this paper. Here, we will simply state that German law expresses that there are specific requirements for an agreement if one of the parties is a layperson. According to "Bürgerliches Gesetzbuch" it is a central feature in the German law that the consumer must be protected. From the other party of the agreement, i.e. the landlord, it is expected that he shows more caution and is better able to take care and protect his own interests – or at least that he has better resources to contact a lawyer to assist him. In German tenancy law, the principle of "contractual freedom" is dominant, which means that the parties can agree on terms and conditions that differ from the terms and conditions set out in the law in their specific contract if they decide to do so. But in many cases the law also states that the terms and conditions cannot be to the disadvantage of the tenant. Consequently, it is not possible to agree on conditions that provide the tenant with poorer conditions than those stipulated by the law. The tenant can have better conditions than those set out in the law, but not more disadvantageous conditions.

The German "Transparenzgebot" – a demand for transparency
The Germany legal system has a "Transparenzgebot" (Henkel 2004, 309-310), a transparency demand. It is explicitly stated in the law that provisions of contracts as well as terms of business must be transparent, i.e. clear and comprehensible. If provisions are not clear and comprehensible, they are considered an excessive disadvantage to one of the parties, and are therefore unenforceable and have no legal implications (§ 307 Bürgerliches Gesetzbuch). The explicit phrase demanding transparency is new in German law, but it derives from a principle that has existed for many years in the legal practice in court. This means that comprehensibility and clarity are seen to be important by the legislature. But what do the terms "clear" and "comprehensible" actually mean? This question is worth discussing, as there might be several interpretations of the words

and principle, and as several strategies might be useful in achieving the required transparency of the provisions. These interpretations originate from the complexity and the duality of the communication situation of contracts.

The double communication situation
The communication situation of the contract is extremely complex, as the contract text must adapt to two different situations simultaneously. In the direct communication situation, the two parties are entering into a contractual relationship, concerning the renting of accommodation. When they affix their signature to the contract, both parties become senders and receivers of the text, and at the same time, through their signature, they achieve rights and obligations towards each other.

In addition to this, an indirect communication situation exists in which the contract must also be operative. This situation will primarily have significance in case a dispute occurs between the parties, e.g. concerning the compliance or non-compliance with the contract or interpretation of the wording of the contract. In this indirect situation the text sender is the lawyer who originally produced the text and the text receiver is the lawyer or legal authority who is to decide in the dispute, often a judge in court. The contract and especially its wording constitute an essential part of the basis on which the legal authority evaluates the dispute. But other sources are likewise considered and taken into account at the decision making (Busse 1992): e.g. the law, previous judicial decisions and judicial literature. In other words, the legal authority integrates the text in a larger hierarchical system of rules originating from different sources in the legal universe.

The double communication situation described above can be visualized as follows:

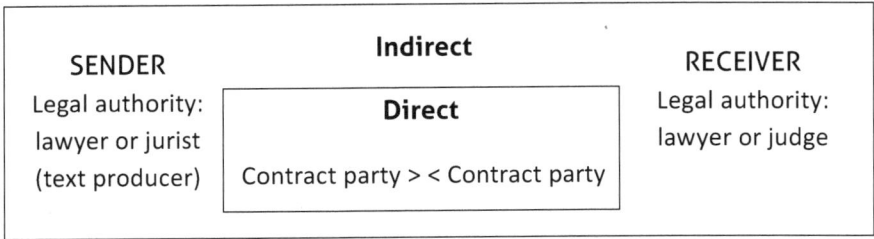

Figure 2: Double communication situation (Larsen 2009; inspired by Faber et al. 1997)

Interaction of communication situation and function

According to Gunnarsson (1982, 2009), the text producer of a *law* text may choose to give citizens first priority. He then focuses on the citizens' possibility of understanding the law text and acting correctly in accordance with it in their various social situations. In this case, the text producer uses the citizen perspective and the action-directing function when he formulates the law text. The other possibility for the text producer is to give lawyers as well as judges and their judging in accordance with the law text in court situations the highest significance, which means that he takes the court perspective and prioritises the control-directing function (Gunnarsson 2009, 105). She argues that this distinction of the perspectives and functions of law texts also applies to "other action-oriented texts" (Gunnarsson 2009, 121), and analysis has shown that this hypothesis is in fact correct when it comes to the genre of legal contracts (Larsen 2009). The text producer can give either the parties in the direct communication situation or the lawyers in the indirect communication situation first priority – by emphasizing the party perspective or the court perspective. The term "party perspective" is chosen as it is a more precise term when we are talking about contract texts than "citizen perspective", which is the term Gunnarsson (2009, 105) uses when talking about law texts. If the court perspective is applied, the most important task of the text is to make it possible for the lawyers and the judge in court to control the actions of the parties. When turning to the party perspective, the text must first and foremost – or at least also – perform the act of giving the parties directions for their actions in order for them to be able to act in accordance with the provisions of the contract. Depending upon which perspective is chosen when formulating the text, the consideration of the layperson's difficulties in understanding the text, due to his lacking text competence, i.e. linguistic and non-linguistic knowledge, is ascribed more or less importance.

Among researchers there is no consensus on whether the contract parties are intended as receivers of a contract or not: e.g. Stengel-Hauptvogel (1997), Fish (2004) and Busse (2004) represent the attitude that the contract parties are not, or only secondarily, the receivers of a contract, whereas Werther and Helmersen (1989) and Gläser (1990, 1993) express that the contract parties are in fact the primary or only receivers of the contract. In my opinion, focussing on *either* the direct communication situation *or* the indirect communication situation will simplify the picture in an inappropriate way. Therefore, Gunnarsson's description of the communication is highly applicable, because it shows the complexity of communication in the legal universe, as well as the importance of the conscious prioritising by the text producer of one or the other perspective and function.

The complexity of communication through legal contracts is made especially apparent when we apply this description; the text must be viable in both communication situations at the same time, but one of the perspectives, and thus one of the communication situations, will be given first priority.

The perspectives and functions of contracts can be visualized in the following way:

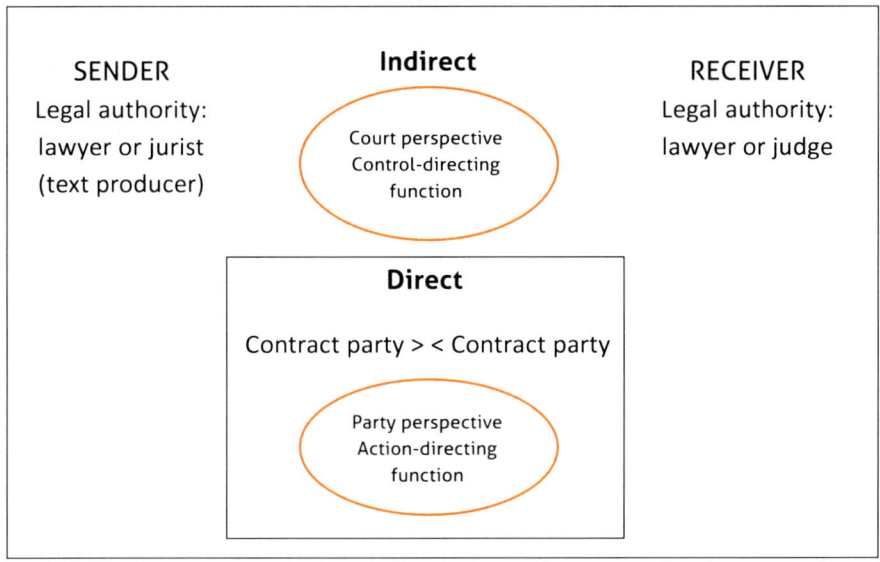

Figure 3: Double communication situation and function (inspired by Gunnarsson 1982, 2009 and Faber et al. 1997)

Two surveys among German lawyers

The two surveys that were carried out in 1998-1999 and 2012 among German lawyers who are formulating contracts on a regular basis gave a clear indication that text producers do indeed make use of these perspectives, although they did not use the actual expressions from Gunnarsson (1982, 2009) "citizen/party perspective" and "court perspective". When asked, it was obvious that the lawyers were highly aware of the linguistic drawing up of the contract, and that a consistent attitude or position is reflected in their individual practices. This is quite interesting and does not correspond with Gunnarsson (2009), as she points out that "linguistic questions are of very little concern to lawmakers" (Gunnarsson 2009, 128)[5].

---

[5] The subjects of Gunnarsson's study were Swedish lawmakers, whereas the subjects of this study were German lawyers. However, the role of nationality and position within the legal universe has not been investigated in either of the studies, so it is not possible to say, whether the reasons for the difference might be found in these aspects.

The results of the two lawyer surveys were that no consensus exists among the lawyers as a group as regards the question raised in the surveys. No common practice is followed by all lawyers: Half of the lawyers responded with an answer that can be summed up as a "no", stating that they formulate contracts in the same way irrespective of the characteristics of the parties; and half of the responding lawyers answered the question with a "yes" or a conditional "yes", indicating that they do, in some cases, formulate contracts differently when one of the parties is a layperson; that other factors also play an important role when they are deciding how to formulate the contract; or that all contracts should be comprehensible to everybody, not only contracts in which one party is a layperson. All lawyers who answered the question expressed reflective arguments for their handling of the parties, e.g. laypeople, in connection with contracts.

Reasons for *not changing* the wording
The most important reasons for formulating a contract in the conventional way, even if a layperson is a party to the contract, can be found in the perspective and the function of the contract. A number of respondents specified in the surveys that they aimed at ensuring legal certainty and clarity; it is of utmost importance to them to be able to predict how the court will interpret a certain word or phrase, and therefore they utilize conventional words and phrases: One of the respondents said that the more formalistically the contract is formulated, the easier it is to predict how the court will interpret it.

The aim of these respondents is to make sure that the judge interprets words and expressions in the right way. They are apprehensive that the judge will assume another content of a word or phrase if for example a non-juridical common word or phrase is used instead of the legal term or phrase, i.e. that a different meaning is derived if the conventional legal expression is not used. The contract must enable the judge to perceive in the most optimal way what is intended. Respondents indicated that in order to achieve this, it can be necessary to use wording that is unreadable or difficult to understand for laypeople – in their own interest. Whether the layperson understands the text or not is less important when the contract is being formulated. This means that the lawyers make use of the phrases and words that have proved to be unambiguous in previous judicial decisions in court, rather than using words that will be easier to understand for the layperson. In this way, they endeavour to meet the demand of the law that the stipulations in contracts must be clear and comprehensible (§ 307 Bürgerliches Gesetzbuch); not necessarily comprehensible to the layperson as a party, but more importantly to the judge who is to decide in case of a dispute between the parties. They prioritize the court perspective in accordance with Gunnarsson (2009) and the control-directing function is of the greatest importance to them. This means that they are primarily oriented towards the indirect communication situation in which lawyers and judges are the predominant text receivers.

Some of the respondents mentioned other reasons for not changing the text, e.g. that they would not like to talk down to the contract parties, thus running the risk of disqualifying the parties' knowledge, that the lawyer himself is proud that he masters the specific legal language. Some rather obscure reasons were also given, such as that some lawyers might wish to make the true contents, limitations or implications of the provisions in the agreement opaque to one of the contract parties in order to bring the other party into a better position (cf. Iversen et al. 1992, 112; Bhatia 1993, 13).

Reasons for *changing* the wording
Other lawyers in the two surveys made it clear that when the lawyer formulates the contract in an unconventional way, his primary reason for doing so is that he is aiming at ensuring comprehensibility in the contract. This means that he is also focusing on complying with the demand of clarity and comprehensibility in the law. Several lawyers stated that they find it sensible and very important that the parties are able to understand the contract without assistance. They also emphasized the importance and the necessity of the lawyers taking the special conditions of the parties into consideration in every single case. These lawyers aim to make sure that the wording of the contract is as comprehensible as possible to the parties in order to avoid uncertainty and disagreement

between the parties and thereby further legal processes. Not only the parties to the contract should be able to understand the agreement, but any citizen; a respondent states that the lawyer should strive at formulating the contract in a way which makes it comprehensible to a normal citizen. This reflects that the party perspective (or even the citizen perspective) (Gunnarsson 2009) is given the highest priority by these lawyers. They take their point of departure in the direct communication situation and see the parties as the primary text receivers, prioritizing the action-directing function of the text.

Strategies applied by the responding lawyers
Some of the responding lawyers did in fact state which strategies they make use of when making an effort to accommodate the lacking linguistic and non-linguistic competences of the layperson. The strategies can to a large extent be retraced in the analyzed 'layperson-friendly' contract text (Deutscher Mieterbund 2013), as opposed to the conventional contract text (Gundeigentum-Verlag 2013), and examples from the former text are therefore given in the following part of the paper (article numbers from the contract are indicated in parentheses with each example). The strategies, stipulated by the lawyers are for example[6]:

A. Explain technical/legal terms and unambiguous legal expressions in the contract text or in an appendix as well as utilize concrete instead of abstract formulations.

1. *"Dies gilt auch für Satellitenempfangsanlagen (Parabolantennen)"* (§ 14, Abs. 4) [„This goes also for satellite receiving systems (parabolic antennas)", my translation]

2. *"...nach Wohnfläche (qm-Zahl)..."* (§ 4, Abs. 2) [„according to living space (number of square metres)", my translation]

---

6 See Larsen (2013) for further examples.

3. *"...soweit wichtige Gründe (Haus- oder Wohnungskauf, Kündigung, Reparaturen) dies erfordern..."* (§ 15, Abs. 1) ["...if important reasons (house or flat purchase, termination, repairs) require this...", my translation]

In examples (1) and (2) we see that rather abstract technical words relating to tenancy have been elaborated briefly with a common or explaining word in parentheses. In example (3) the legal expression "wichtige Gründe" ["important reasons", my translation], which is a conventional expression in German legal language for the reasons for which a legal step can be taken, is specified and made concrete by mentioning what reasons have been established as "important reasons" in previous judicial decisions and judicial literature, although there is no explicit reference to these sources in the text. The instances are not marked as examples, but as a full list of reasons, given in parentheses. However, in other articles in the same contract we find the expression "wichtige Gründe" used without any explanation (e.g. § 18, Abs. 1 and 2), especially about the complicated regulations for terminating the tenancy without notice; explanations are therefore not being used consistently as a strategy throughout the text to assist the layperson.

B. Use generally comprehensive words and descriptions as well as non-formal language.

4. *"Zusätzlich zur Miete bezahlt der Mieter..."* (§ 3, Abs. 2) ["In addition to the rent the tenant pays...", my translation]

The word "bezahlen" ["pay", my translation] is a neutral, comprehensible word from everyday language, whereas a word such as "entrichten" ["disburse", my translation] is a formal word, mostly used in departmental style (Duden 1993, 925). The formal word is often seen in legal contracts, but in this contract we see the neutral, everyday word.

C. Use (relatively) simple sentence structure, i.e. to a less extent use "periodic style", in which all information on a particular theme is placed in one period; this is the style which characterizes legal language (Engberg 1999).

5. *"Übernimmt der Vermieter beim Auszug des Mieters dessen Einbauten oder bauliche Veränderungen, so hat er dem Mieter die nachgewiesenen Kosten zu erstatten, abzüglich eines angemessenen Abschlags für Abnutzungen."* (§ 9, Abs. 8) [„If, when the tenant is moving out, the landlord takes possession of the fixtures or the constructional modifications made by the tenant, [then] he must compensate the tenant for the documented costs, deducting a reasonable reduction for abrasion", my translation]

In example (5) we see a rather simple sentence structure (for a legal text) consisting of a preceding conditional sentence with inversion and a matrix sentence, marked by the word "so", followed by a sentence-substituting adverbial phrase in the form of a prepositional group beginning with "abzüglich". In most contracts, sentence structures can be very extensive, due to the use of "periodic style", but in this contract it seems that the text producer has made an effort to avoid this style, for example through the use of analogy as in example (1), indicating that a previous rule is applicable also for the item mentioned in the following sentence.

D. Avoid excessive insertions, references and empty phrases.

6. *"Die Kündigungsvoraussetzungen richten sich im Übrigen nach den gesetzlichen Vorschriften und den vertraglichen Absprachen (siehe §§ 8, 17-22 dieses Vertrages)."* (§ 2) ["All other termination conditions are regulated in accordance with the provisions of the law and the agreements of the contract (cf. §§ 8, 17-22 of this contract)", my translation]

In legal language, intertextuality conventionally plays a great role as the contract is incorporated into a larger universe of texts and the knowledge of the lawyer when he produces the text. This is a context which constitutes an immense system of texts and knowledge (primarily relating the contract to laws, previous judicial decisions and juridical literature), as the contract text itself is only one of the items drawn on when the judge decides in case of a dispute between the parties. In the layperson-oriented contract analyzed for this paper, no attempts have been made to avoid references. Actually, several external references can be found in the text, although it was stated by respondents in the surveys that they are trying to avoid external references. These references are either rather concrete external references to sections of the law or internal references to other articles in the same contract text – as shown in example (6). There are, however, also some external non-concrete references to the law, e.g. "nach den gesetzlichen Vorschriften" ["in accordance with the provisions of the law", my translation] – as also shown in example (6). In cases like these the law, or part or concrete section of the law referred to is not mentioned, although Bürgerliches Gesetzbuch (2003) consists of 2385 sections. This makes it very difficult for the reader, especially the layperson reader, to understand the actual content of the text: He receives the information that a law stipulates regulations concerning the theme in question, and that this is considered sufficiently important to be mentioned, but he is left to his own devices as regards deciding if he needs to know the content of the regulations, as well as finding the regulations if he considers this necessary. The text in example (6) concerns the conditions of terminating the tenancy, and as the conditions for this must be rather important for the tenant, it can be seen as particularly inexpedient that his access to information is impeded in the way described.

E. Explain the content of the provisions orally to the parties before they sign the contract.

Giving oral explanations to the parties in connection with the signing of the contract seems to be a non-optimal solution, partly because the explanation provided will probably often be forgotten rather soon, partly for the reason that in case individuals other than the person who heard the oral explanation enter into the contract, e.g. a new spouse or an heir, the information will be lost. This entails a risk of disputes between the parties (eventually at court) about the interpretation of the content.

The text producer's dilemma
A dilemma arises for the text producer: He must make a choice and prioritize if he is to let the party perspective or the court perspective be predominant, i.e. giving the text a primarily action-directing or a control-directing function; should he enable the parties to understand what their

actions must be in order to comply with the provisions of the agreement, or enable the court and the judge to control the actions of the parties and decide if they have fulfilled their obligations towards each other? The choice has implications for the focus of the contract: with the party perspective, the text producer is focusing on comprehensibility and legal certainty, and with the court perspective, focus is on legal clarity – and legal certainty as well.

Furthermore, an enhanced comprehensibility might – at least in the eyes of some lawyers – lead to less legal certainty and clarity, but on the other hand, better comprehensibility might also lead to an increase in the legal certainty of the parties.

Conclusion
In this paper, it has been discussed which types of text competence are necessary in order to enable the layperson to understand the contract. We saw that it is necessary for the layperson to possess knowledge of and understand "the language we use", for instance the legal lexis: e.g. legal terms, phrases and expressions, abstract formulations as well as formal expressions. Furthermore, he should understand the legal syntax, i.e. the sometimes complex sentence structure, resulting from the conventional use of "periodic style" and insertions. He also needs to be able to cope with legal references, more or less explicit, precise and elaborate. Last, but not least, he should be able to understand the deeper legal implications of the linguistic elements – based on non-linguistic "knowledge about the world we talk about", primarily the law, previous juridical decisions and judicial literature, as the contract text is embedded in a large legal system of texts and knowledge.

This study has investigated the strategies used by text producers to meet the lack of text competences of the layperson. The surveys among German lawyers practicing contract production in their daily work, as well as the text analysis of two German contracts have demonstrated some interesting results concerning the strategies of the lawyers. At the lexical level, the lawyers explain legal terms and unambiguous legal expressions in the contract text or in an appendix to the contract and also attempt to use concrete instead of abstract expressions, generally comprehensible notions and descriptions and formally unmarked expressions. At the syntactic level, the lawyers make an effort to use (relatively) simple sentence structures and avoid excessive insertions and empty phrases. Furthermore, they often explain the content of the contract orally to the parties before the latter are to sign this. The last strategy mentioned by the lawyers was avoiding exact and inexact references to external sources, such as the law, and references internally to other parts of the contract text itself. This strategy was not, however, found in the text analyzed for this paper. Further research will be needed to examine if this is in fact a general tendency.

Finally, the surveys also showed that half of the lawyers considered the party perspective and the action-directing function important; they were, under certain conditions, willing to take the lacking text competence of one of the parties into consideration when producing a contract text. The remaining lawyers did not find it possible or appropriate to adapt the contract wording to a layperson, because some of them did not see the parties as receivers of the contract at all, or not primarily; they were focussed on the court perspective and the control-directing function of the text. As for the analyzed 'layperson-friendly' text, this remains a text using a perspective comparable to the "law-conventional citizen perspective" that Gunnarsson presents (2009, 121). There is still a long way to go before obtaining a text with a "natural citizen perspective" which is seen by Gunnarsson (2009, 122) as "the necessary next step". This would involve a "radical reconstruction" of the text (Gunnarsson 2009, 122), taking the citizens' – or in this particular case the parties' – use of the text as a point of departure. It remains to be seen, however, if such an all-encompassing reconstruction would receive a positive response in the German legal universe, from judges, lawyers and contract parties, and whether the resulting text would be seen as an acceptable legal text.

References

Bhatia, Vijay K. 1993. *Analysing Genre: Language Use in Professional Settings.* London/New York: Longman.

Bürgerliches Gesetzbuch. In der Fassung der Bekanntmachung vom 2. Januar 2002 (BGBl. I S. 42 ber. S. 2909 und BGBl I 2003 S. 738). 2003. dtv 5001. Sonderausgabe unter redaktioneller Verantwortung des Verlages C.H. Beck oHG München: Deutscher Taschenbuch Verlag.

Busse, Dietrich. 2004. Verstehen und Auslegung von Rechtstexten – institutionelle Bedingungen. In *Die Sprache des Rechts. Recht verstehen*, edited by Kent D. Lerch, 7-20. Berlin/New York: de Gruyter.

Busse, Dietrich. 1992. *Recht als Text. Linguistische Untersuchungen zur Arbeit mit Sprache in einer gesellschaftlichen Institution.* Tübingen: Niemeyer.

Dam, Helle V. and Jan Engberg. 2005. Introduction. In *Knowledge Systems and Translation,* edited by Helle V. Dam, Jan Engberg, Heidrun Gerzymisch-Arbogast, 1-13. Berlin/New York: de Gruyter.

Deutscher Mieterbund. 2013. „Wohnungs-Mietvertrag". Accessed May 30, 2013. http://www.mieterbund.de/download.html.

Ditlevsen, Marianne Grove, Jan Engberg, Peter Kastberg and Martin Nielsen. 2007. *Sprog på arbejde. Kommunikation i faglige tekster.* 2. udg. Frederiksberg: Samfundslitteratur.

Engberg, Jan. 1993. "Prinzipien einer Typologisierung juristischer Texte". *Fachsprache* 15: 31-38.

Engberg, Jan. 1998. *Introduktion til fagsprogslingvistikken.* Århus: Systime.

Engberg, Jan. 1999. "Die dänischen Fachsprachen im 20. Jahrhundert und ihre Erforschung: eine Übersicht". In *Fachsprachen. Ein internationales Handbuch zur Fachsprachenforschung und Terminologiewis-

senschaft, edited by Lothar Hoffmann, Hartwig Kalverkämper and Herbert Ernst Wiegand. 1564-1570. HSK 14.2. Berlin/New York: de Gruyter.

Faber, Dorrit, Mette Hjort-Pedersen, Dorte Madsen and Joan Tournay. 1997. *Introduktion til dansk juridisk sprogbrug – metoder og analyser*. København: Handelshøjskolens Forlag.

Gläser, Rosemarie. 1990. *Fachtextsorten im Englischen*. Tübingen: Narr.

Gläser, Rosemarie. 1993. "A Multi-level Model for a Typology of LSP Genres". *Fachsprache* 15: 18-26.

Grundeigentum-Verlag. 2013. "Mietvertrag für Wohnräume". Accessed May 30, 2013. http://www.grundeigentum-verlag.de/ge-09.01.php3.

Gunnarsson, Britt-Louise. 2009. *Professional Discourse*. London/New York: Continuum.

Gunnarsson, Britt-Louise. 1982. *Lagtexters begriplighed*. Lund: LiberFörlag.

Henkel, Alexandra. 2004. "Inhaltskontrolle von Finanzprodukten nach der Richtlinie 93/13/EWG des Rates über missbräuchliche Klauseln in Verbraucherverträgen." Juristische Reihe TENEA. Vol. 76. PhD diss. Rheinische Friedrich-Wilhelms-Universität Bonn. Berlin: TENEA Verlag für Medien. Accessed May 30, 2013. http://www.jurawelt.com/sunrise/media/mediafiles/13769/tenea_juraweltbd76_henkel.pdf.

Iversen, Bent, Jørgen Nørgaard, Morten Wegener and Niels Ørgaard. 1992. *Lærebog i Dansk og International Erhvervsret*. Charlottenlund: Jurist- og Økonomforbundets Forlag.

Kvam, Sigmund, Karen Patrick Knutsen and Peter Langemeyer. 2010. "Text in Context". In *Textsorten und kulturelle Kompetenz. Interdisziplinäre Beiträge zur Textwissenschaft. Genre and Cultural Competence. An Interdisciplinary Approach to the Study of Text* edited by Sigmund

Kvam, Karen Patrick Knutsen and Peter Langemeyer. 21-33. Münster/New York/München/Berlin: Waxmann.

Larsen, Aase Voldgaard. 2013. "Wissensvermittlung in Verträgen – Eine empirische Untersuchung der Repräsentation und Nicht-Repräsentation von Wissen in deutschen Mietverträgen". In *Die Rechtssprache in der internationalen Diskussion* edited by Marina Wagnerová and Gerald G. Sander. 59-76. Hamburg: Verlag Dr. Kovač.

Larsen, Aase Voldgaard. 2009. "Faglighed og forståelighed i kontrakter. En undersøgelse af sproglige forskelle i tyske lejekontrakter rettet mod henholdsvis fagmand og lægmand". PhD diss., Aalborg University. Accessed May 30, 2013. http://vbn.aau.dk/da/publications/faglighed-og-forstaaelighed-i-kontrakter(0177b810-3310-11deb107-000ea68e967b).html.

Lux, Friedemann. 1981. *Text, Situation, Textsorte. Probleme der Textsortenanalyse, dargestellt am Beispiel der britischen Registerlinguistik. Mit einem Ausblick auf eine adäquate Textsortentheorie.* Tübinger Beiträge zur Linguistik 172. Tübingen: Narr.

Sarangi, Srikant. 2001. "On demarcating the space between 'lay expertise' and 'expert laity'". *Text.* 21, 1-2: 3-11.

Stengel-Hauptvogel, Ina. 1997. *Juristisches Übersetzen Spanisch – Deutsch. Immobilienkaufverträge.* Tübingen: Narr.

Werther, Charlotte and Ole Helmersen. 1989. *Konflikt eller konsensus.* København: Handelshøjskolen.

White, James Boyd. 1982. "The Invisible Discourse of the Law: Reflections on Legal Literacy and General Education". *Michigan Quarterly Review.* Vol. XXI, No. 3: 420-438.

Instructional Semantics and linguistic competence

Lotte Dam

> *In the case of knowing a language, by common consensus what counts is being able to use it fluently and appropriately, not being able to apply conscious and analytic categories to it. Only linguists have declarative knowledge of how language works; (Harder 2007, 19)*

Abstract
Linguistic competence concerns a speaker's ability to create meaningful utterances by means of linguistic expressions, as well as a hearer's ability to decode linguistic expressions and create meaning. In this sense, from the point of view of the speaker, linguistic expressions are the building blocks for conveying meaning, and, from the point of view of the hearer, the informational source for creating meaning. The purpose of this paper is to contribute to a deeper understanding of how linguistic meaning is produced and understood in communication. It is argued that the Theory of Instructional Semantics provides an operative framework for explaining this process. The paper also explores the consequences that this approach can have in a didactic context.

Introduction

As both speakers and hearers, humans apply, and benefit from, their linguistic competence in communication.[1] The competence concerns a speaker's ability to create meaningful utterances by means of linguistic expressions, and a hearer's ability to decode linguistic expressions and create meaning.[2] In any communicative situation, the speaker applies his or her linguistic competence to express a meaning through an utterance, and the hearer applies his or her linguistic competence to create a meaning.[3] Between the speaker and the hearer is language, which the parties make use of as a medium of communication.[4] Language works as a medium of communication because of its inherent properties: its constituents have meaning, which, by means of different combinations, creates meaningful utterances. It seems relevant to identify more accurately the relation between these properties and linguistic competence. I believe that the theory of Instructional Semantics can be applied to identify this relation.

The framework of Instructional Semantics takes a cognitive approach to meaning, in the sense that meaning is identified with conceptualization.[5] Meaning is seen to be constructed dynamically in an interpretive process by individual interlocutors. This process is initiated by linguistic

---

1 In this paper, *speaker* refers to both an oral speaker and a writer, and *hearer* refers to both a listener and a reader.
2 The term *linguistic competence* is used in a more general sense of the word than that advocated by Chomsky, who opposes it to *linguistic performance* (Chomsky 1965, 4). Like Paradis (2003), among others, I believe that Chomsky's rather restrictive use of the expression makes it impossible to describe powerful general principles that govern language use. Instead, I use Paradis' (2003, 15) definition of competence in Cognitive Semantics as referring to the language users' ability to adequately construct and fully understand expressions by means of language itself and additional resources such as memory, intentionality, general knowledge, etc.
3 For a more detailed discussion of a general theory of communication, see for example Sperber and Wilson (1986).
4 In the oral communication, the actors of course also make use of gestures/mimics, intonation, etc.
5 Langacker (2000) highlights the difference between a cognitive and a formal conception of semantics.

expressions from a speaker in a context in which an utterance is produced. In this sense, linguistic expressions are seen as clues (or input) to an interpretive process.

After providing a description of Instructional Semantics, I will proceed to add a section on second language acquisition. Linguistic competence is used in communication between various speakers of a language, but it is also used by students of a foreign language. This paper suggests that Instructional Semantics can contribute to the improvement of linguistic competence in a foreign language.

Instructional Semantics
According to Instructional Semantics, linguistic input is thought of as instructions for the hearer to perform an act of interpretation. The approach is based on semantic constructivism, which presupposes an intervening level between language and reality, created by the meaning of language in the sense that language helps structure conceptual space (see Thrane 1998, 42), and is inspired by well-known theories in the field of cognitive linguistics, such as Evans (2006), Fauconnier (1994), Johnson-Laird (1983), Langacker (1987, 1991, 2000), and Talmy (2000).

The more specific instructional approach to meaning construction has been applied more or less explicitly by different scholars. The theory has been described by Thrane (1997, 1998, 1999), Boye (2007), Harder (1996, 2007) and Dam and Dam-Jensen (2007), among others, whereas it has been applied more directly in linguistic analyses by for example Thrane (1997), Dam (2008, 2012), and Dam and Dam-Jensen (2010).

The interpretive process results in the creation of mental representations (see Fauconnier 1994). In the words of Boye (2007, 69): "Instructions may be seen as instructions to establish mental representations, and the establishment of mental representations may be seen as the product of following linguistic instructions". The interpretative process is performed automatically, or subconsciously, by virtue of language competence.

Instructional Semantics rests on the assumption that an utterance consists of three phases: input, process and product (Harder 2007; Dam and Dam-Jensen 2007). The input for the process is language. Language can be seen as a toolbox from which the speaker can select relevant linguistic tools with the aim of conveying a specific meaning. Once an utterance has been produced, an interpretive process is initiated in the hearer's mind. The product of this interpretive process is the establishment of meaning (output).[6] The following model illustrates the creation of linguistic meaning, and is at the same time a reflection of both the speaker's and the hearer's linguistic competences, as the speaker applies his competence in his selection of input, and the hearer applies his competence in the interpretive process:

input [the speaker's use of language] → *process* [the hearer's interpretation of language] → *product (output)* [the hearer's creation of meaning]

I will illustrate this process with an example from Harder (2007, 22):

1. *He smiled* = declarative (past (smile (he)))

To explain the input of this simple utterance in instructional terms, Harder (2007, 22) formulates the following paraphrase, giving one instruction for each content element: "Identify the referent of 'he', predicate the concept 'smile' of him, apply the model to the past situation that we are talking of, and take that as providing a factual representation of that situation."[7] These instructions are input for the interpretive process, and the output is the "final" meaning of the utterance, consisting of a mental representation in the hearer's mind.

In Instructional Semantics, linguistic items are thought to contribute to the interpretive process in different ways, depending on whether they are functional or lexical. The traditional distinction between function-

---

6   The term *meaning* is used about both the input, i.e. the semantics of the linguistic items, and about the result of the interpretive process, i.e. the product/output.

7   The notational system used in Harder's example illustrates the different linguistic elements, but obviously not the instructions themselves.

al and lexical items – or between open and closed classes – allows a systematic account of the way in which linguistic expressions contribute to the interpretive process, depending on their categorial status. As pointed out by Dam and Dam-Jensen (2007, 84), if we want to make systematic statements about linguistic meaning, we must assume that when they use linguistic expressions, language users comply with conventions that are stable enough to make such systematic statements possible. In the following paragraph, I will describe more accurately how lexical and functional items, respectively, contribute to the creation of meaning.

Functional and lexical items
To explain the difference between lexical and functional items, I will take example (1) as my starting point. As Harder (2007, 23) points out, content elements such as 'he' and 'smile' introduce what might be called the more 'substantial' elements – the elements that form key constituents of the output-level understanding – whereas 'past' and 'declarative' are not focal constituents of output understanding.[8] Another important point made by Harder (2007, 23) is that, whereas the key constituents (the lexical items) provide the substantial content, the functional elements are 'purely procedural', i.e. they do not add substance of their own. However, we would not have access to the substantial elements if it were not for the procedural elements (Harder 2007, 23-24). Along the same lines, Givón (1995, 343) argues that "[...] overt grammatical signals – syntactic constructions, morphology, intonation – cue the text processor, they *guide* him/her in the construction of a coherent mental representation of the text...". Linguistic expressions are clues from a speaker to a hearer, and the functional items in particular constitute the driving forces of the process.

Functional items
Functional items do not provide instructions about themselves; rather, they provide guidelines for the interpretive process by giving instructions about the interpretation of something which is distinct from themselves, typically lexemes. The verbal categories, for example, provide

---

8   In Harder's example a pronoun is used, but a noun would probably better illustrate a content element.

instructions about the temporality (tense), modality (mood) and delimitation (aspect) of a verbal situation denoted by a lexeme, in this case a verb. In (1), for example, the past tense suffix instructs the hearer to understand a situation of smiling in a past context. Another example for illustration is the definite article attached to a noun. According to Harder (2007, 22), the definite article signals that the hearer should understand the nominal phrase (NP) headed by *the* as representing a referent that must be identified.[9] In other words, the definite article introduces a referent in a mental representation.

An important characteristic of a functional item is that it is univocal: its meaning is always the same. Thrane (1999, 23) phrases the idea of univocality in this way, "The semantic effect that a linguistic item has in virtue of being a carrier of **structural** meaning is **always** the same." This is called the principle of uniformity of semantic effect. The idea that the meaning of a functional item is always the same does not mean, however, that its input cannot lead to different types of output. The above-mentioned instruction of the definite article suggested by Harder (2007, 22) (the definite article signals that the hearer should understand the NP headed by *the* as representing a referent that must be identified) can both lead to what is known as definite specific reference and definite generic reference, depending on the co- and/or context. In other words, the same input can lead to two different (although related) outputs:

2. The lion came out of its den.

3. The lion is a mammal.

Apart from these two overall types of reference, traditional classifications of reference include reference subtypes, such as for example anaphoric and situational reference. Assuming univocal meaning has the advantage that multiplying beyond necessity may be avoided, as counting with more than one definite article would imply a number of preexisting different

---

9   Harder assumes the DP-analysis, i.e. that the determiner is the syntactic head. This analysis is widely accepted, and for example Abney (1986), Longobardi (1994), Hewson (1991), and Eguren (1989) have argued in favour of this.

meanings, for instance based on different referential types (see Thrane 1997, 238-239). This would implicate a taxonomic problem consisting in determining an exact number of meanings of the definite article.

Another example of how to analyze functional items is offered by Dam and Dam-Jensen (2010), whose object of study is mood in Spanish. It is argued that mood, in general, carries information about spatial orientation. This has to do with the speaker's conceptualisation of reality, defined as the speaker's conceptualisation of the situation of utterance. Formulated at a general level, the indicative in Spanish prompts factual situations, whereas the subjunctive prompts either non-factual situations or presupposed factual situations. In order to capture both of these meanings, the instructional value of the subjunctive must be formulated in rather general terms. Based on ideas from Mejías-Bikandi (1998), Dam and Dam-Jensen (2010, 125-126) propose the following univocal instructional meaning of each modal form that would account for the appearance of the modal forms in different contexts:

- Indicative: locate the situation created by the verb relative to the situation of utterance.

- Subjunctive: do not locate the situation created by the verb relative to the situation of utterance.

Factual situations are linked to the situation of utterance (indicative), whereas non-factual situations are not (subjunctive). The instructional meaning of the subjunctive captures presupposed factual situations, because a situation which is already linked to the situation of utterance does not need an instruction to be linked.

It is a basic characteristic of functional items that they belong to paradigms. The indicative, the subjunctive and the imperative, for example, belong to the paradigm of mood. The instructional value of each modal form should be formulated in such a way that it accounts for the affinity between the different members of the paradigm. In more general terms, when attempts are made to formulate an instructional meaning for the different functional items, this should be done in such a way that all the members of the paradigm will subscribe to the same general characteristics of that paradigm.

When a paradigm has only two members, their meanings will normally form a kind of oppositional relation, i.e. a meaning dichotomy. An example of this is the position of the attributive adjective in Romance languages, which is sometimes placed before a noun, and sometimes after a noun. As the position of the adjective is a structural phenomenon, it can be considered a functional item with a corresponding functional meaning in terms of instructions. Dam (2008) presents a hypothesis of Spanish adjective placement which suggests that the postnominal position of an adjective instructs a hearer to create focus on the adjective, whereas the prenominal position of the adjective does not.[10] Many grammars of Spanish describe a number of different empirical facts separately, for example the prototypical position of certain adjective classes, without explaining the relation between the meaning of the adjectives and the meaning of its prototypical position.[11] Dam (2008) argues that a large number of empirical facts, not only regarding specific adjective types, but also regarding typical positions in specific text types, for instance, can be predicted, and thereby explained, on the basis of an instructional meaning of the two positions.[12]

Paradigms vary with regard to complexity of the contexts in which their members may appear. Whereas the contexts in which pre- and post-position of Spanish adjectives are clearly delimited, those of other paradigms are more complex as their members may be employed in a greater variety of linguistic settings. In these cases it is not altogether simple to formulate an instruction. An example of an item whose meaning is not easy to pin down is the Spanish *se*, which may not always be a reflexive

---

10   As this example illustrates, in some cases one of the parts of a dichotomic relation is formulated negatively on the basis of the other part.
11   Examples are Salvá (1988, 326 ff.) and Gómez Torrego (2002, 60), who present a description of the contexts that prototypically invite pre- or post-position, but do not explain why.
12   In the same vein, Thrane (1997, 238) points out that many descriptive English grammars offer detailed instructions for the *use* of the articles in English, whereas they do not usually say anything about what the articles mean *in themselves*.

pronoun, as it contributes to very different meanings, which cannot all be considered reflexive as such. This is illustrated by the following examples, in which REFL is used in a "neutral" way to illustrate that the same linguistic expression can contribute to very different meanings:

4. Pedro no se ha afeitado esta mañana.
   Pedro not REFL shave-PRF DEM morning
   'Pedro did not shave this morning.'

5. Pedro no se ha levantado.
   Pedro not REFL get up/rise-PRF
   'Pedro has not got up yet.' / 'Pedro has not risen.'

6. Pedro se durmió muy tarde.
   Pedro REFL sleep-PST very late
   'Pedro fell asleep very late.'

7. Este año, no se han vendido muchas casas.
   DEM year, not REFL sell-PRF many houses
   'This year, not many houses have been sold.'

There may be a historically explainable link between the different uses of *se* in Spanish (there are even more meaning variants than those illustrated here), but from a synchronous point of view, the meaning of the various instances is very different, and so are the syntactic contexts in which *se* occurs. As pointed out in Maldonado (2008, 156), "one must question whether the reflexive is the general construction from which other uses can be derived". In keeping with this statement, I will argue that a univocal meaning is not operational in this case. To account for this, I will complement Instructional Semantics with some basic ideas from Construction Grammar (CG).

In general terms, in the realm of CG, a construction is a pairing of a form and a meaning, which is manifested as a type of linguistic expression with a specific meaning content. It is a sign which can be of a lexical as well as a syntactic nature (Goldberg 1995, 7). As is well-known, different scholars have contributed to the theory of CG in different ways, i.e. CG is not one single theory. Some of the important contributions are Fillmore, Kay and O'Connor (1988), Goldberg (1995, 2006), Croft (2001) and Fried and Östman (2005).

More recent contributions take a usage-based approach to CG, such as Brenier and Michaelis (2005), Stefanowitsch (2004) and Gries (2005). Within these developments of CG, corpus analysis is used as a tool to reveal schematic patterns of pairings of form and meaning, with the aim of identifying constructions and describing them. I would argue that a corpus analysis of contexts in which *se* forms part, would not result in the discovery of completely new construction types. Different types have already been identified and described separately in grammar books.[13] Consequently, there is broad consensus that we are dealing with different constructions with different meanings, i.e. conventionalized pairings of form and meaning.

As already explained, in Instructional Semantics it is assumed that the functional items themselves carry instructions (e.g. mode morphemes). In the case of *se* I will argue, however, that an instructional meaning must be connected to an entire construction, and not only to *se* itself, due to the fact that it is possible to extract a set of constructions with a rather fixed set of properties which must be present for the specific meaning of *se* to occur. I suggest that the idea of several pairings of form and meaning and the notational system of CG are adequate for describing different constructions.

As reflexivity (again used in a "neutral" sense) is very complex in Spanish, and it is not the main subject of this paper, I will not present a detailed outline of the entire reflexive system (such as how many types exist), but merely outline the main idea in general terms.

Following the ideas presented in Maldonado (1992, 2008), I suggest a *se* as a middle voice marker as opposed to a merely reflexive *se*.[14] Based on

---

13   I am aware of the fact that it is possible to find new uses in the language, but here I refer to genuinely new construction types.
14   Consult Kemmer (1993) for a detailed characterization of the category of middle voice.

the idea that the crucial function of the middle voice marker is to highlight the affectedness undergone by an experiencer (Maldonado 2008, 155), Maldonado accounts for a large number of different but related meanings, such as readings of unexpectedness and inchoative readings. Another function of Spanish *se* is to mark impersonality, such as in (7). This meaning can also be related to the middle voice; however, as the meaning is quite different, I will categorize it as a different function.

Following the ideas presented, the structures of examples (5)-(7) can be tentatively illustrated as follows:[15,16]

[[SBJ] [REFL (all persons)] [V-INTR]]
[[SBJ (animate) [REFL (all persons)] [V-TR]]
[[REFL (3SG)] [V-TR (3SG)] [S (-HUM)]]

These descriptions constitute only the form of the pairings of form and meaning. The reading of (5) involves a reading of a change in position caused by the initiative of the referent of the subject himself, the reading of (6) involves a change of state (sleep → fall to sleep) which *happens* to the referent of the subject, and the reading of (7) involves an impersonal meaning. Within Instructional Semantics, these meanings should be formulated as instructions which are connected to the entire constructions.

After this description of the functional items, including the basic idea of a single instructional meaning connected to a functional item complemented by basic ideas from CG with regard to larger pairings of form and meaning, I will now address the meaning of lexical items.

---

15 The reason why the illustrations are described as tentative is that other restrictions may exist than those indicated. In the first constructions, there is, for example, a restriction regarding the verb, as not any kind of intransitive verb can be used, but only a fixed group. These verbs could be indicated in the description of the construction, but it is also a possibility that in the theory of CG, each of these verbs would be seen as forming part of its own construction.

16 I do not suggest a representation of (4) as I think that *se* in this case is a functional item itself and does not form part of a larger unit.

Lexical items
In instructional semantics, the meaning of lexical items is also instructional, but not in the same sense as that of functional items. It was suggested above that an NP headed by the definite article introduces a referent in a mental representation, but it was not explained how the meaning of the noun contributes to the establishment of meaning. A lexical item is instructional in that it provides instructions to establish a mental representation of its own (substantial) meaning, i.e. of the entity, situation, etc. that the lexeme denotes. If the definite article heads the noun *car*, the hearer is told to create a mental representation of the lexeme *car* for the referent of the NP *the car*. In this case, the mental representation is of an entity (as opposed to for example a situation or a property represented by other types of lexical items).

Lexical meanings are described in dictionaries. Nevertheless, a word does not evoke the same meaning in all individuals. According to Thrane (1997, 241), individuals have private concepts for words. This means that a difference may exist from one individual to another between the concepts attached to a lexeme. Typical examples are differences in meaning evoked in an adult and a child, or in an expert and a layperson, but vast differences may also appear between individuals in general. However, since meaning is conventional, and people in a language community generally understand one another, there must be a kind of core meaning which people share – a *public* meaning.

Since interlocutors do not have access to other people's concepts of a word, the concept which is evoked when a speaker utters a word as part of a communication, is not his or her concept, but the hearer's own concept (although he or she may, in some cases, know that the speaker's concept may to some extent differ from their own).

The dynamics of meaning
A consequence of the view of language presented above is that there is not a one-on-one relationship between input and output, as the output is not fixed until after the hearer's interpretation process of the input. For this reason, I prefer Thrane's (1997, 238; 1999, 23) "dynamic" counterpart (A) to the traditional principle of compositionality (Cann 1993, 4) (B):

A: The semantic effect of a complex expression is a function of the semantic effects of its parts, plus the semantic effects of the structural rules by which it is composed.

B: The meaning of an expression is a monotonic function of the meaning of its parts and the way they are put together.

Thrane's principle of compositionality takes into account the fact that the output meaning is not merely the sum of fixed meanings of the input parts, but rather a result of different instructions that serve as information for the interpretative process. This is what is meant by *dynamic*. In the case of the definite article, this means that the output meaning, i.e. the definite specific type of reference, is not settled until the interpretive process has been completed, whereas the input meaning of this functional item is a broader (instructional) meaning. In Harder's (2007, 13) words, "The understanding of meaning as subacts (...) implies that linguistic meanings are different in kind from the complete interpretations that they are designed to give rise to."

Up to this point, I have only proposed that linguistic items form part of the input for the hearer's interpretation. However, as is well-known, linguistic meaning is not the only type of input on which the hearer draws. The hearer not only follows the instructions from the linguistic items, but he or she also draws on information from co- and context.

Let us return to the NPs in (2) and (3). In both examples, the hearer is instructed to establish a referent, and, as it is only possible to create reference to entities which are already introduced in the discourse universe, the hearer will "look around" for at relevant referent. In (2), the combination of the past with the lexical meaning of the verb *crawl out* and the specific meaning of place, *its den*, prompt specific reference, whereas the predicate of *a mammal* makes generic reference salient. In some other cases, the cotext does not suffice, and the hearer will have to look for information in the situation, the context, to interpret an utterance or part of it. (2) and (3) are void of context here, and can only be interpreted by their cotext, but in reality they would be part of a context.

It would be profitable to integrate the dynamic understanding of the establishment of linguistic meaning and thereby linguistic competence in a didactic context. In this paper I suggest that Instructional Semantics be integrated in a comprehension-based second language acquisition theory as a basis for grammar teaching. I will describe these ideas in the following paragraph.

Didactic perspectives
It is a recognized fact within research on second language acquisition (SLA) that the acquisition of a second language (L2) in the classroom differs from the acquisition of a first language (L1) (although some branches of SLA attempt to make up a type of natural setting), as the two types of language acquisition involve linguistic competence in quite different ways.[17] One difference is that the competence which is used in grammar classes is of a more intellectual character than the more natural language competence.

There has been an ongoing discussion in the field of SLA as to whether or not explicit grammar instruction matters at all (Dam, 2011). In this article, I will not enter this discussion, but take as a premise that grammar instruction is useful for second language learning. It goes without saying that if explicit grammar instruction matters, it is important to know what it takes to teach foreign language grammar as efficiently as possible. The integration of Instructional Semantics in a comprehension-based second language acquisition theory which constitutes a basis for grammar teaching assumes that the acquisition of the functional items of a foreign language presupposes a deep understanding of the systematic semantics of each form before using them, i.e. reception before production.[18] This means that the focus is in the first place shifted from the students'

---

17   Here *Second Language (Acquisition)* refers to any language learned after the mother tongue, synonymously with *target langue*. This means that I do not distinguish between *second* and *foreign* languages. *Acquisition* is used in a more general sense without distinguishing between *acquisition* and *learning*.
18   See for example VanPatten and Cadierno (1993a, 1993b) and Ellis (1993) for more details about the comprehension approach.

linguistic output to their learning and acquisition with the aim of increasing their further output abilities. This shift away from the students' linguistic output to their comprehension requires awareness with respect to the make-up of grammar classes, specific activities, exercises, etc.

Rather than describing an infinite number of detached meanings of the same grammatical item, the grammar teacher ought to explain (apparent) different instances with a starting point in a core meaning: the instructional meaning. As mentioned earlier in this paper, Dam (2008) presents a hypothesis of Spanish adjective placement according to which the postposition of an adjective instructs an interlocutor to create focus on the adjective, whereas the preposition of the adjective does not create this focus. According to this hypothesis, these single meanings explain a large number of different empirical facts, and making this explicit is presumed to facilitate the students' ability to understand these empirical facts and possibly enhance their own ability to use the placement of the adjective more correctly. The assumption behind this is that students are able to relate different – and also more particular – instantiations of a functional item to one core meaning. Another example is mood in Spanish, also mentioned as an example earlier in this article. As mentioned, the indicative in Spanish prompts factual situations, whereas the subjunctive indicates either non-factual situations or presupposed factual situations. Some grammars describe the mood system in terms of government. Some linguistic expressions are (almost) always followed by a verb in the subjunctive, and in such cases it might be useful to learn this by heart. Nevertheless, in the longer run, for the majority of students it is not possible to memorize the mood system in Spanish, one reason being that several linguistic expressions both allow the indicative and the subjunctive. The proposed instructional meaning of the subjunctive explains why the subjunctive gives rise to both non-factual situations and presupposed factual situations. It also explains many other empirical facts, for example the so-called government and the reason why several linguistic expressions allow both the indicative and the subjunctive.

Different methods may be used in the classroom to make explicit the meaning of functional items. The teacher may explain the subject at hand on the basis of examples in which the functional item appears in a reduced contextual setting. In this situation, the advantage of working with smaller contexts is that the risk of disturbances in the interpretation process is minimized, as context tends to blur the meaning of the functional item because it may evoke different mental representations.[19]

Another possibility is to invite the students to formulate grammatical rules themselves. By way of induction, students are confronted with a number of authentic linguistic examples, each representing the same grammatical phenomenon. The students are then asked to induce the semantic grammatical value: the core meaning.

After having made explicit the meaning of a functional item, the teacher can proceed to carry out reception noticing activities (instead of the more traditional fill-in exercises). This may be done, for example, by showing the students a large number of authentic examples in which the functional item appears. Confronted with the examples, the students are asked to explain how the meaning of a specific functional item works in a specific context, and to explain the implications for the final meaning in each specific example. This activity focuses on the interaction between the instructional meaning of a specific functional item and the co- and/or context. These examples should at first represent standard language usage, but later on when the students seem to have grasped the core meaning, examples of more unusual usages can be included. Metaphorically speaking, the language student builds a type of radial network of usage types, in a sense akin to Lakoff's radial categories (Lakoff 1987, 91). The idea that the meaning of the functional items is always the same does not entail that these items are not flexible and cannot appear in unexpected contexts, creating special nuances. By means of the progressive integration of more peripheral usages, the students gradually learn how more "special" meanings may occur depending on the specific context. This will provide them with a more complete understanding of an item, which in the long run will facilitate a more varied and precise output.

It is a large pedagogical advantage of the instructional approach to the meaning of functional items that it avoids taxonomic problems; students

---

19   With regard to more complex cases such as reflexivity in Spanish, the focus point will be how to recognize the specific construction.

are not invited to enumerate how many types of each functional item exist, as there is only one single meaning. It can also be assumed that students will be more conscious of the meaning of co- and context.

In addition to the mere grammar acquisition, I believe that it is important to increase the students' consciousness about the creation of linguistic meaning. Meaning is not established prior to language, but is created *through* language.

Concluding remarks
Instructional Semantics is a theory which seems to be useful to account for the way in which language works as input for the establishment of linguistic meaning in a systematic, precise and homogeneous way. It does so, for instance, by using the division of linguistic items into functional and lexical items, each of which has its own type of instructional meaning. In addition to the language itself, a speaker and a hearer are participants in the process of establishing linguistic meaning. In this process they apply their linguistic competence. In any communicative situation, the speaker applies his or her linguistic competence to express a meaning through an utterance, and the hearer applies his or her linguistic competence to understand this meaning.

However, linguistic competence is not only applied in daily communication between speakers of a language, but it is also applied by students of a foreign language. Instructional Semantics seems to be operational as an integrated part of a comprehension-based second language acquisition theory for the improvement of linguistic competence in a foreign language. I have suggested integrating Instructional Semantics as a basis for grammar teaching. This integration assumes that the acquisition of the functional items of a foreign language presupposes a deep understanding of the systematic semantics of each form before using them. This means that focus in grammar classes is moved away from the students' linguistic output to their learning and acquisition, with the aim of increasing their further output abilities. This shift to the students' comprehension will have consequences for the make-up of grammar classes, specific activities, and exercises.

References

Abney, Steven. 1986. "Functional elements and licensing". Paper presented to GLOW 1986. Gerona, Spain.

Boye, Kasper. 2007. "Semantic complexity vs. conceptual complexity". In *Language and Comprehension: Input, Process, Product (Acta Linguistica Hafniensia* 39), edited by Kasper Boye, 69-82. Copenhagen: C.A. Reitzel.

Brenier, Jason M., and Laura A. Michaelis. 2005. "Optimization via Syntactic Amalgam: Syntax-Prosody Mismatch and Copula Doubling". *Corpus Linguistics and Linguistic Theory* 1: 45-88.

Cann, Ronnie. 1993. *Formal Semantics*. Cambridge: Cambridge University Press.

Chomsky, Noam. 1965. *Aspects of the Theory of Syntax*. Cambridge, Massachusetts: The MIT Press.

Croft, William. 2001. *Radical Construction Grammar. Syntactic Theory in a Typological Perspective*. Oxford: Oxford University Press.

Dam, Lotte. 2008. "La posicion del adjetivo atributivo español. Un enfoque instruccionalista sobre la nocion de focalizacion." *Español Actual* 89: 7-37.

Dam, Lotte. 2011. "Teaching and acquiring second language grammar at the university." In *Policies, Principles, Practices: New Directions in Foreign Language Education in the Era of Educational Globalization*, edited by Rita Cancino, Lotte Dam, and Kirsten Jæger, 93-113. Cambridge: Cambridge Scholars Publishing.

Dam, Lotte. 2012. "Modusformerne i spansk - rumlig eller ikke rumlig forankring". *Ny Forskning i grammatik* 19: 29-46. Odense: Syddansk Universitet.

Dam, Lotte, and Helle Dam-Jensen. 2007. "Instructions, context and compositionality: How to combine functional, lexical and interpretive dimensions of meaning." In *Language and Comprehension: Input, Process, Product* (*Acta Linguistica Hafniensia* 39), edited by Kasper Boye, 83-100. Copenhague: C.A. Reitzel.

Dam, Lotte, and Helle Dam-Jensen. 2010. "Mood in complementizer phrases in Spanish: How to assess the semantics of mood." *Pragmatics & Cognition* 18(1): 111-135. John Benjamin's Publishing Company.

Eguren, Luis. 1989. "Algunos datos del español en favor de la hipótesis de la frase determinante". *Revista Argentina de Lingüística* 5(1-2): 163-203.

Ellis, Rod. 1993. "Interpretation-based grammar teaching". *System* 21: 69-78.

Elman, L. Jeffrey, Elizabeth A. Bates, Mark H. Johnson, Annette Karmiloff-Smith, Domenico Parisi and Kim Plunkett. 1996. *Rethinking Innateness. A connectionist perspective on development.* Cambridge/Massachusetts/London: The MIT Press.

Evans, Vyvyan. 2006. "Lexical concepts, cognitive models and meaning construction". *Cognitive Linguistics* 17(4): 491-534.

Fauconnier, Gilles. 1994. *Mental spaces.* Cambridge: Cambridge University Press.

Fillmore, Charles, Paul Kay, and Mary O'Connor. 1988. Regularity and idiomaticity in grammatical constructions: the case of *let alone*. *Language* 64: 501-538.

Fried, Mirjam, and Jan-Ola Östman (eds.). 2005. *Construction Grammars. Cognitive grounding and theoretical extensions.* Philadelphia: John Benjamins Publishing Company.

Givón, Talmy. 1995. *Functionalism and grammar*. Amsterdam/Philadelphia: John Benjamins Publishing Company.

Goldberg, Adele. 1995. *Constructions: A Construction Grammar Approach to Argument Structure*. Chicago: Chicago University Press.

Goldberg, Adele. 2006. *Constructions at Work: The Nature of Generalization in Language*. Oxford: Oxford University Press.

Gómez Torrego, Leonardo. 2002. *Gramática didáctica del español*. Madrid: Ediciones SM.

Gries, Stefan Th. 2005. "Syntactic Priming: A Corpus-based Approach". *Journal of Psycholinguistic Research* 34(4): 365-399.

Gries, Stefan Th., and Anatol Stefanowitsch (2004). "Extending collostructional analysis: A corpus-based perspective on 'alternations'". *International Journal of Corpus Linguistics* 9 (1): 97-129.

Harder, Peter. 1996. *Functional Semantics. A Theory of Meaning, Structure and Tense in English*, Moutin de Gruyter, Berlin.

Harder, Peter. 2007. "Shaping the interactive flow. Language as input, process and product". In *Language and Comprehension: Input, Process, Product (Acta Linguistica Hafniensia, 39)*, edited by Kasper Boye, 7-36. Copenhague: C.A. Reitzel.

Hewson, John. 1991. "Determiners as heads." *Cognitive Linguistics* 2(4): 317-337.

Johnson-Laird, Philip N. 1983. *Mental models*. Cambridge: Cambridge University Press.

Kemmer, Suzanne. 1993. *The middle voice*. Amsterdam: John Benjamins Publishing Company.

Lakoff, George. 1987. *Women, Fire, and Dangerous Things*. Chicago and London: The University of Chicago Press.

Langacker, Ronald. 1987. *Foundations of Cognitive Grammar, vol. 1.Theoretical Prerequisites.* Stanford: Stanford University Press.

Langacker, Ronald. 1991. *Foundations of Cognitive Grammar, vol. II. Descriptive Application.* Stanford: Stanford University Press.

Langacker, Ronald. 2000. "Why a mind is necessary. Conceptualization, grammar and linguistic semantics". In *Meaning and Cognition*, edited by Liliana Albertazzi, Liliana, 25-38. Amsterdam: John Benjamins Publishing Company.

Longobardi, Guiseppe. 1994. "Reference and proper names: A theory of N-movement in syntax and logical form". *Linguistic Inquiry* 25(4): 609-665.

Maldonado, Ricardo Soto. 1992. "Middle Voice: The case of Spanish SE". PhD diss., University of California. Maldonado, Ricardo Soto. 2008. "Spanish middle syntax: A usage-based proposal for grammar teaching". In *Cognitive Approaches to Pedagogical Grammar*, edited by Sabine De Knop and Teun De Rycker, 155-196. Berlin: Mouton De Gruyter.

Mejías-Bikandi, Errapel. 1998. "Syntax, discourse and acts of the mind: a study of the indicative/subjunctive contrast in Spanish". PhD diss., University of California.

Paradis, Carita. 2003. Is the notion of *linguistic competence* relevant in Cognitive Linguistics? *Annual Review of Cognitive Linguistics* 1: 207-231. Amsterdam: John Benjamins Publishing Company.

Salvá, Vicente. 1988. *Gramática de la lengua castellana.* Madrid: Arco Libros.

Sperber, Dan, and Deirdre Wilson. 1986. *Relevance. Communication and Cognition.* Oxford/Cambridge USA: Blackwell.

Talmy, Leonard. 2000. *Toward a Cognitive Semantics. Vol. 1: Concept Structuring Systems.* Cambridge: The MIT Press.

Thrane, Torben. 1997. "Sounds, Structures and Senses". In *Essays presented to Niels Davidsen-Nielsen on the Occasion of his Sixtieth Birthday*, edited by Carl Bache, and Alex Klinge, 235-250. Odense: Odense University Press.

Thrane, Torben. 1998. "Nominaler, nominaliseringer og semantisk kompleksitet". *Hermes* 21: 39-66.

Thrane, Torben. 1999. "Understanding Functionality". Unpublished paper presented at The Polish Academy of Science, Krakow, May 1999.

VanPatten, Bill, and Teresa Cadierno. 1993a. "Explicit Instruction and Input Processing". *Studies in Second Language Acquisition* 15(2): 225-243.

VanPatten, Bill, and Teresa Cadierno. 1993b. "Input Processing and Second Language Acquisition". *The Modern Language Journal* 77(1): 45-57.

Performance and competence in usage-based construction grammar

Kim Ebensgaard Jensen

Abstract
While formalist approaches to language in the Chomskian tradition distinguish sharply between performance and competence in their modeling of language competence, performance and competence are considered to be in a mutually influential relation in usage-based models of language. Language competence, in the latter approach, is, much like in Dell Hymes' notion of communicative competence, held to be experientially based in the sense that speakers establish their competence through inductive social-cognitive processes of schematization and conventionalization. Making a case for the usage-based definition of the language system, this paper explores the interplay between performance and competence in the [V *until* ADJ]-construction in a construction grammar perspective in which grammatical constructions are considered meaningful symbolic units on par with lexemes. Based on an investigation of a section of the *Corpus of Contemporary American English*, the present study takes into account empirically observed internal and external patterns of usage in the description of this linguistic phenomenon and provides a usage-based constructional overview of the competence pertaining to this construction. The purpose of the present study

is thus two-fold, aiming to provide a communicatively plausible account of this particular phenomenon and to show that, indeed, no satisfactory description of the construction which ignores performance-based data would be possible, as the construction itself is very much defined by external properties such as specific genre and register affiliations and a quite specific communicative function.

Introduction
Theoretical linguistics traditionally assumes a sharp distinction between the language system and language use. This is reflected in Chomsky's (1965) **competence-performance** and in Saussure's (1983, 14) **langue-parole** dichotomies. **Competence** and **langue** both refer to the language system itself as an abstract entity. **Performance** and **parole** are both used with reference to language use in social and communicative contexts. While separating langue from parole, Saussure's (1983, 9-10) conception of the language system is nonetheless communicatively plausible to some extent, as he acknowledges the social reality in which language exists, while Chomsky completely isolates competence from any type of social or communicative context (Chomsky 1965, 3). The relationship between this knowledge of language structure and actual language performance is one of unidirectional influence with competence determining performance. Consequently, naturally occurring language data are useless in the description of language competence, such data being "fairly degenerate in quality" (Chomsky 1965, 31). In other words, performance has no place in linguistic theory.

However, there are several syntactic phenomena which cannot be satisfactorily described without reference to performance-based factors, because their linguistic functions are intertwined with specific social, situational, and communicational contexts. The present paper provides an analysis of such a phenomenon – namely, the [V *until* ADJ]-construction as in 'Fry until crisp' or 'Whisk until smooth'. It is argued that this particular construction serves the very specific purpose of providing instructions in terms of how to manipulate ingredients when preparing a dish, such that the construction typically appears in recipes and the register associated with this genre. If one wants to provide an explicit and communicatively relevant account of a linguistic phenomenon, the notion of competence must be changed such that it allows the linguist to take into account relevant contextual features. It would simply not be possible to describe [V *until* ADJ] in a framework based on a conception of competence that excludes how, when, and where the construction is used.

Realizing the need for a socially and communicatively more relevant conception of language competence, Hymes (1972, 53-73) suggested the idea of **communicative competence,** which is a speaker's ability to use language in general, and includes both structural and socio-cultural knowledge associated with the language system. This does not necessarily mean that these are not distinct types of knowledge, but they are both integral components of an individual's knowledge of how to use language. For instance, it is an individual's knowledge of socio-cultural practices that forms the individual's knowledge of the contextual and situational contexts in which certain structures are appropriate. Such information must, if one is interested in language as a means of communication, be taken into account in the description of linguistic phenomena. This requires the researcher to observe language performance, because it is through actual language use that we can witness how language interacts with context; it is through observing this interaction that linguists can reconstruct, as it were, communicative competence. Communicative competence calls for performance being taken seriously and advocates the feasibility of using naturally occurring language data in the description of the language system (Hymes 1972, 63-67), as patterns of actual use are likely to reflect contextual information associated with structures in the language system itself. Knowledge of contexts in which certain structures have certain functions is likely to be stored in the language system as competence associated with the structures in question. Hymes' notion of communicative competence lays, in many ways, the foundation for **usage-based linguistics** (Kemmer and Barlow 2000; Bybee and Hopper 2001) which takes a step further from Hymes' (1972) idea, accepting a conception of linguistic competence in which it is based on language performance. Here, the language system is experientially based via observing and engaging in linguistic interaction with other speakers of the language in question and structured through a number of cognitive processes. In one variant of usage-based linguistics,

usage-based construction grammar (e.g. Tomasello 2003), the language system consists of networks holistic symbolic structures, or constructions, combining structural, conceptual, and socio-cultural information.

Drawing on the framework of usage-based construction grammar, the present paper explores the interplay between competence and performance in our analysis of the symbolic structure of [V *until* ADJ], making the point that language competence is influenced by language performance to the extent that linguistic phenomena cannot be satisfactorily described without taking into account patterns in performance. Thus, the purpose of this paper is two-fold. Firstly, it serves to provide a communicatively relevant and realistic account of [V *until* ADJ]. Secondly, it serves to show that, in order to do so, we must draw on a conception of competence in which performance is given a central role.

The paper is organized as follows. First, the reader will be introduced to usage-based construction grammar through a brief overview of the principles of **usage-based linguistics** and **construction grammar**. The main empirical method of analysis, **collostructional analysis**, will then be introduced and put to use. This is followed by a discussion of the results of the analysis and what they reveal about the form-content structure of the construction, and by discussions of patterns of illocutionary value, transitivity, and temporality which shed further light on the communicative function of the construction. Pervading the analysis of the construction is, of course, the interaction between performance and competence, which is fundamental to our overall analysis.

Usage-based construction grammar
As mentioned above, the usage-based view of language (Kemmer and Barlow 2000; Bybee and Hopper 2001) is closely related to Hymes' communicative competence, since competence in usage-based models includes various types of contextual information. Competence is further considered to be influenced by performance. The language system is experientially based on usage-patterns, as "structure, or regularity, comes out of discourse and is shaped by discourse in an ongoing process." (Hopper 1998, 156). Language competence emerges from, and is estab-

lished on the basis of, recurring patterns; the schematic structures that are found in the language system are based on **schematizations** over recurring structures in actual discourse:

> [...] for usage-based theorists the fundamental reality of language is people making utterances to one another on particular occasions of use. When people repeatedly use the same particular and concrete linguistic symbols to one another in "similar" situations, what may emerge over time is a pattern of language use schematised in the minds of users as one or another kind of linguistic category or construction. (Tomasello 2003, 99)

Tomasello (2003, 145,169-73) calls this process **functionally based distributional analysis**. Once emerged, the system licenses further instances of language use. Frequency is important in the establishment of linguistic structures in an inductive experiential process of **conventionalization**: "each time a word (or construction) is used, it **activates** a node or a pattern of nodes in the mind leading to its ultimate storage as a conventional grammatical unit" (Croft and Cruse 2004, 292 – boldface in original). Langacker (1987, 59) argues that linguistic structures fall "along a continuous scale of entrenchment", and that "[e]very use of a structure has a positive impact on its degree of entrenchment whereas periods of disuse have a negative impact". Thus, there is an intimate relation between linguistic structures and **usage-events**, described by Kemmer and Barlow (2000, ix) as "instances of a speaker's producing and understanding language". Since the language system is usage-based, one may logically assume that regularities in context will be stored in the language system: "[s]ituations and their participants are also repetitive phenomena, and linguistic routinization is ultimately inseparable from cultural practices in general" (Bybee and Hopper 2001, 21).

Our description of [V *until* ADJ] is a constructionist one, as we employ the descriptive and theoretical apparatus associated with construction grammar (Fillmore 1988, Fillmore et al. 1988, Goldberg 1995, Croft 2001) in which the language system does not consist of abstract syntactic combinatorial rules, but of taxonomic networks of **constructions**.

A construction is a symbolic unit which pairs linguistic form with conventionalized meaning, and the constructional networks of language are organized in accordance with general cognitive processes and structures, rather than the autonomous purely syntactic processes and structures posed in Chomskian linguistics. Constructions may be formally simple, consisting of just one element, or formally complex, consisting of more than one element. In complex constructions, the multi-unit formal configuration is itself associated with conventionalized meaning. Thus, individual lexemes are technically also constructions; indeed, Bergen and Chang (2005, 145) inform us that "linguistic knowledge at all levels, from morphology to multi-word units can be characterized as constructions, or pairings of form and meaning." This view reflects "one of the fundamental hypotheses of construction grammar: there is a **uniform representation of all grammatical knowledge** in the speaker's mind, in the form of generalized constructions" (Croft and Cruse 2004, 255 – boldface in original). Construction grammar is essentially a semiotic discipline in which all linguistic forms are associated with some type of content. In that respect, competence in construction grammar probably has more in common with Saussure's langue than Chomsky's language competence. An important feature of the symbolic nature of constructions is that the conventionalized content of a construction features both semantics and pragmatics (Goldberg 1995, 7). The semantics-pragmatics interface is a contested area, and accounting for it in detail would be beyond the scope of this paper. Suffice it to say that a general distinction is made between semantic (propositional or conceptual) content and pragmatic (contextual or usage-generated) meaning in traditional linguistics. In this dichotomy, semantic content is considered conventional and internal to the language system, while pragmatic meaning is considered to be external to the language system and not covered by language competence. Construction grammar moves pragmatic information into the sphere of conventionalized content, and making it part of the language system and individual speakers' linguistic competence. Croft (2001, 19) informs us that the content of a construction covers "the properties of the situation described by the construction", "the pragmatic situation of the interlocutors", and "the properties of discourse in which the utterance is found". Constructions may thus be described as having **internal properties**, covering internal structure, and **external properties**, covering "the properties of the construction as a whole, that is to say, anything that speakers know about the construction that is relevant to the larger contexts in which it is welcome" (Fillmore 1988, 36). The external properties of a construction capture the contextual knowledge that Hymes' (1972) notion of communicative competence was designed to include into the language system.

Having dealt with the basics of usage-based linguistics and construction grammar respectively, we can now address the basics of usage-based construction grammar. Croft (2005, 274) provides a usage-oriented definition of a construction as "an entrenched routine [...] that is generally used in the speech community [...] and involves a pairing of form and meaning". Usage-based construction grammar allows for redundancy and complex delicacy in the constructional networks in tandem with Tomasello's (2003, 145,169-73) above-mentioned principle of functionally based distributive analysis. It is characteristic of usage-based construction grammars that the constructional network includes **item-class-specific** and **item-specific** constructions (Croft 2003, 57-58; Tomasello 2003, 139), the former being constructions in which schematic slots revolve around specific lexical classes, and which have specific communicative functions; the latter refers constructions that evolve around just single lexical items and have specific communicative functions. Allow me to draw on some of my own research as a source of examples here. In Jensen (2012), it was shown that the Danish [V *ihjel*]-construction covers a number of subconstructions with more or less specific communicative purposes. Whenever the V-position is filled by 'slå' (HIT or BEAT), the construction invariably refers to the generic act of KILLING SOMEONE, making [SLÅ *ihjel*] an item-based subconstruction. The construction also subsumes a number of subconstructions which are item-class-based. For instance, when members of the semantic class of verbs of ingestion appear in the V-position the construction serves to express situations in which the MAIN PARTICIPANT CAUSES ITS OWN DEATH BY INGESTING EXCESSIVE AMOUNTS OF FOOD. When members of the semantic class of verbs of effort appear, the construction expresses situations of a PRIMARY PARTICIPANT INVOLVED IN SUCH HARD WORK THAT IT RESULTS IN THE PRIMARY PARTICIPANT'S DEATH.

Due to the relation of mutual influence between competence and performance in which performance determines competence and competence informs performance, investigating performance is the key to the understanding of language competence. Usage-based descriptions of a linguistic phenomenon must be based on naturally occurring discourse data, as patterns of use mirror the language system itself. One methodological framework that is useful in this respect is **corpus linguistics**, which involves combinations of qualitative and quantitative investigations of principled databases of naturally occurring language, called **language corpora**. Corpus linguistics is useful in the identification of **association patterns**: "the systematic ways in which linguistic features are used in association with other linguistic and non-linguistic features" (Biber et al. 1998, 5). Association patterns are extremely important in the description of the language system, because they give the analyst hints as to the linguistic and non-linguistic information stored in the language system. Observing association patterns is vital in the identification of both internal and external properties of constructional entities.

Method: collostructional analysis
Our usage-based study of [V *until* ADJ] is based on observations of association patterns in the 20,445,868-word 2011-section of Davies' (2012) *Corpus of Contemporary American English* – henceforth *COCA* – a corpus of naturally occurring American English from the year 2011. Our usage-based description of [V *until* ADJ] should not be taken to be an exhaustive and final statement about the construction, but it does provide valuable information on the construction in the form of a fairly firm generalization. We must, however, keep in mind the possibility that there is more to say about the construction, because there may be patterns of use that are simply not captured in the 2011-section of *COCA*. Moreover, the generalization proposed may be tested against further data and falsified or verified, thus ultimately serving as a type of empirically based hypothesis.

The major type of quantitative analysis used in the present study is what Stefanowitsch and Gries (2003; 2005) call collostructional analysis, which measures the lexical association patterns of a construction and lexemes that appear in it. The main premise is formulated as two fundamental principles:

- The **principle of semantic compatibility**: "words can (or are likely to) occur with a given construction if (or to the degree that) their meanings are compatible" (Stefanowitsch and Gries 2005, 4).

- The **principle of semantic coherence**: "since a word in any slot of a construction must be compatible with the semantics provided by the construction for that slot, there should be an overall coherence among all slots" (Stefanowitsch and Gries 2005, 11).

Semantic patterns among the lexical items attracted to a construction may thus provide the analyst with an idea of what the constructional semantics might be.

We shall make use of two variants of collostructional analysis in the present study: **simple collexeme analysis** which measures the attraction of a lexeme to a construction, and **covarying collexeme analysis** which measures the co-attraction of two lexemes within the same construction.

Simple collexeme analysis (Stefanowitsch and Gries 2003) operates with four input frequencies: the occurrence of the lexeme in the construction, the occurrence of the lexeme in all other constructions, the occurrence of all other lexemes in the construction, and the occurrence of all other lexemes in all other constructions:

Table 1: Simple collexeme analysis

	Lexeme	Other lexemes	Row totals
Construction	x	a	x+a
Other constructions	y	b	y+b
Column totals	x+y	a+b	column totals + row totals

The total sum is run through a Fisher Exact Test (Pedersen 1996) or a similar statistical test (for some alternative tests, see Stefanowitsch and Gries 2003, 238-239), yielding a *p*-value, which constitutes the **collo-**

struction strength of attraction of the lexeme to the construction; the higher the *p*-value the stronger the attraction.

Covarying collexeme analysis (Stefanowitsch and Gries 2005) also operates with four input frequencies: the occurrence of the first lexeme in one position in the construction, the occurrence of all other lexemes in the same slot, the occurrence of the second lexeme in the other slot in the construction, and the occurrence of all other lexemes in the other slot of the construction:

Table 2: Covarying collexeme analysis

	Lexeme 2 in slot 2	Other lexemes in slot 2	Row totals
Lexeme 1 in slot 1	x	a	x+a
Other lexemes in slot 1	y	b	y+b
Column totals	x+y	a+b	column totals + row totals

The total sum is also run through a Fisher Exact Test or a similar statistical test, yielding a p-value, indicating strength of the co-attraction of the two lexemes in the construction in question.

Using Gries (2007), I subjected [V *until* ADJ] to three collostructional analyses:

- simple collexeme analysis of the attraction of lexemes to the V-slot

- simple collexeme analysis of the attraction of lexemes to the ADJ-slot

- covarying collexeme analysis of the co-attraction of lexemes in the V-slot and lexemes in the ADJ-slot

This allows us to address, in isolation and in comparison, attraction patterns in the schematic slots in the constructional template, thus providing us with important indications of the semantic functions of both slots and the relationship between them.

Simple collexeme analysis of the V-slot

In total, 69 lexemes appear in the V-slot in the 2011 section of the *COCA*; they are all listed here:

(1) bake, beat, blanch, blend, boil, braise, break, broil, brown, chill, churn, combine, cook, cool, cut, dry, expand, fork, freeze, fry, glaze, grill, grow, heat, hold, immerse, keep, knead, mash, melt, microwave, mix, nest, place, press, process, pull, pulse, puree, reduce, refrigerate, re-heat, return, rinse, roast, salt, saut, sear, simmer, sit, soak, soften, sand, stand, steam, stir, stir-fry, store, sweat, swirl, toast, toss, turn, whip, whirl, whisk, whiz, wilt, work.

The majority of lexical items in the V-slot belong to a specific semantic class of verbs that we, in an admittedly rather ad hoc fashion, could call verbs of cookery. The fact that the V-slot is dominated by such lexemes suggests that the construction is primarily used in the description of cooking scenarios that involve the manipulation of an ingredient as part of preparing a dish. For instance, 'microwave' predicates the process of heating an ingredient in a microwave, and 'melt' predicates the process of causing an ingredient to change from a solid state to a fluid state by heating it, while 'refrigerate' predicates the process of placing an ingredient in a fridge to lower its temperature. Thus, these verbs express various specifications of a schematic scenario that we will call the ingredient preparation frame,[1] in which a cook engages in an act of preparation directed at an ingredient:

COOK → ACT OF PREPARATION → INGREDIENT

In more general terms, the COOK is a type of AGENT and the INGREDIENT is a type of PATIENT. This structure is part of a matrix of frames which we could simply call the COOKING frame, which covers various generalizations of acts that are involved in the preparation of a meal. The V-element thus displays the behavior of an item-class-specific construction whose schematic element is restricted to members of a specific semantic class of verbs.

---

1   For more on semantic frames, see Fillmore (1982).

Our simple collexeme analysis provides us with a fine-grained view of the function of the V-slot, taking into account frequency of occurrence of lexemes in the V-slot. This table offers a ranking of the 30 most attracted lexemes – they are ranked and accounted for in terms of frequency of occurrence in the corpus (= 'L corpus'), frequency of occurrence in the construction (= 'L construction'), and collostruction strength (= 'CollStrength'):

Table 3: Top 30 attracted items in the V-slot (log-likelihood)[2]

Rank	Lexeme	L corpus	L construction	CollStrength
1	cook	1421	172	2543.2488136958
2	bake	644	91	1363.36600018116
3	saut	156	40	649.087856679974
4	whisk	392	40	568.351962317863
5	beat	1601	38	425.949840249938
6	heat	372	30	411.013060752841
7	stir	1532	34	376.293234363189
8	process	446	22	278.807456720272
9	puree	37	15	259.487946479337
10	roast	215	15	200.65426479407
11	grill	167	14	192.604240526648
12	microwave	67	11	167.030751752012
13	chill	172	12	160.470204880830
14	refrigerate	148	11	148.525454495313
15	blend	366	12	141.900070332377
16	fry	115	9	122.460221317100
17	boil	297	10	118.760700442303
18	simmer	327	10	116.806552822011
19	blanch	35	5	74.3691628010375
20	steam	45	5	71.6830816403067
21	toast	174	6	71.5121027002396
22	soften	313	5	51.8084454520857
23	mix	999	6	50.4212991924076

---

2 Having run the data through both a Fisher Exact Test and a log-likelihood test (Dunning 1993), I decided to apply the latter because it allows for more fine-grained decimal distinctions between the most attracted items.

24	whirl	109	4	48.1695674999113
25	freeze	634	5	44.7305759640135
26	broil	44	3	39.935023324867
27	pulse	65	3	37.5265212953434
28	cut	4363	6	32.9269885548153
29	whip	376	3	26.8994160940135
30	stir-fry	37	2	25.6627009244376

With a collostruction strength nearly twice as large as that of the second-most attracted item 'bake', 'cook' is significantly attracted to the construction. It makes sense that 'cook' should have this specific status in a construction like [V *until* ADJ], given that 'cook' expresses the **basic level category** action of PREPARING FOOD BY HEATING IT, thus capturing numerous different scenarios of preparing food by heating it in various types of cookware. A basic level category is a category which provides information generic enough for the category label to capture a range of different phenomena, but at the same time specific enough to impose a number of restrictions on the phenomena to be included in the category. Croft and Cruse (2004, 83) list the following characteristics of basic level categories: the basic level is (i) "the most inclusive level at which there are characteristic patterns of behavioral interaction", (ii) "[t]he most inclusive level for which a clear visual image can be formed", (iii) "the most inclusive level at which part-whole information is represented", and (iv) "the levels used for neutral everyday use". These features arguably all apply to 'cook'. Essentially, it is left up to the reader to infer, on the basis of the co-text and general encyclopedic knowledge of cookery, the specific type of cooking involved. The generic nature of 'cook' makes it particularly compatible with the semantics of the V-slot in the construction. The strong attraction of 'cook' to the construction also indicates that, in American culture, ingredient preparation via heating is particularly common.

The verb items in Table 3 can be grouped together in semantic categories based on semantic commonalities. For instance, the following verbs express various acts of HEATING OF INGREDIENTS and may be placed under the same semantic category of verbs:

(2) verbs expressing HEATING OF INGREDIENT
    cook, bake, saut, heat, roast, grill, microwave, fry, boil, simmer, blanch, steam, toast, broil, stir-fry

Another fairly strongly represented semantic class in the top thirty of attracted items covers verbs that express various ACTS OF MANIPULATION OF INGREDIENT CONSTITUTION – more importantly, they express scenarios in which the INGREDIENT undergoes a CHANGE OF STATE in terms of its CONSTITUTION such that it has a different CONSTITUTION when the act is complete:

(3) verbs expressing MANIPULATION OF INGREDIENT CONSTITUTION
    whisk, beat, process, puree, blend, soften, whirl, mix, pulse, cut, whip

Of course, this category could be divided into further subcategories in terms of the RESULTANT STATE of the INGREDIENT. For instance 'process' and 'puree' express acts which result in a LIQUID STATE OF CONSTITUTION of the INGREDIENT, while 'cut' results in a STATE OF MULTIPLEXITY, and 'whip' and 'whisp' result in a STATE OF FLUFFINESS. It is also possible to lower the temperature of an INGREDIENT as part of the preparation of a meal, and this is reflected by a semantic class which is not very strongly represented in the top thirty:

(4) verbs expressing lowering of temperature of an ingredient
    refrigerate, chill, freeze

It is worth noting, although we will not pursue this further, that there are only four verbs of this type in the V-slot in the corpus (the fourth one is 'cool' which ranks at 36).

The last class of verbs represented in the top thirty subsumes verbs that express MANIPULATION OF THE SPATIAL LOCATION AND CONFIGURATION OF AN ENTITY, but not necessarily its CONSTITUTION, the only member represented in the top 30 being 'stir'. Stirring is, of course, an activity that is very common in cooking so it should not be surprising that it is fairly strongly attracted to this construction. It should be mentioned that this class is more strongly represented outside the top thirty by verbs such as, for instance, 'toss', 'immerse' and 'place'.

Virtually all of the verbs in these categories can be argued to be more or less specialized terms in the terminology of cookery, suggesting that the construction is closely associated with the register of cookery.[3] Although the classes singled out above express different types of acts involved in cookery, they have one thing in common. They all express varying degrees of telicity, predicating ingredient preparation situations in which the ingredient undergoes a change of state. This is quite obvious in (2-4). 'Stir' is the odd man out in that it does not display telicity as clearly as the verbs in (2-4) – still, not all entities return to their initial states when stirred.

Interestingly, our collostructional analysis also reveals aspects of the culture of cookery in an American context, as the lexemes in the V-slot reflect common methods of INGREDIENT PREPARATION in American cookery. Also, the V-slot draws on the reader's encyclopedic knowledge of cooking, since, in order to understand the instructions in which [V *until* ADJ] is used, the reader must actually know which actions, or methods, the lexemes in the V-slot signify. This suggests that instances of this construction draw not only on language-specific competences, but also on competences associated with cookery.

Simple collexeme analysis of the ADJ-slot
The table below gives a ranked overview of the 30 most attracted items in the ADJ-slot:

Table 4: Top 30 attracted items in the ADJ-slot (log-likelihood)

Rank	Lexeme	L corpus	L construction	CollStrength
1	smooth	821	127	1935.06954928982
2	tender	495	94	1469.46855062709
3	brown	1393	88	1168.96991703839

---

[3] The 'expand'-'strong' covariant pair seems a strange combination. The explanation is that the two co-occur in atypical instances of the construction in the corpus, such as 'David *expanded* his standing among his fellow Israelites until strong enough to rise against his Philistine masters', which is neither an instruction nor an instance of cookery discourse.

4	golden	1157	77	1029.79557710478
5	fragrant	124	26	409.452063050227
6	hot	3276	34	324.314851694815
7	soft	1336	23	242.393151625368
8	creamy	210	17	232.712198988923
9	crisp-tender	18	12	224.590275968538
10	crisp	219	16	215.584909013357
11	ready	2695	23	210.000731829166
12	crumbly	29	9	149.665968757806
13	foamy	18	8	140.22579932284
14	translucent	78	9	129.803196849299
15	firm	129	8	104.984543429229
16	opaque	86	7	95.7989980743017
17	fluffy	89	7	95.2988540550411
18	cool	1805	10	82.4835628899269
19	shimmering	73	6	82.2264738319536
20	spoonable	6	4	74.816345913228
21	crispy	70	5	67.0550235521566
22	warm	1666	8	63.6842074652007
23	pink	867	7	62.9718952346007
24	fork-tender	9	3	50.3795378913987
25	thick	1257	6	47.674272331553
26	syrupy	19	3	45.2632916901495
27	dry	1590	6	44.8703035694200
28	frothy	29	3	42.5476627688484
29	bubbly	65	3	37.5265212953434
30	well-browned	3	2	37.4023168299459

All items on this list express physical attributes with adjectives of TEX-TURE, adjectives of COLOR and COLOR-LIKE ATTRIBUTES, and adjectives of TEMPERATURE being particularly salient. This indicates that the communicative function of the ADJ-slot is to specify the PHYSICAL CONSTITUTION that the INGREDIENT enters into as a result of the COOK's actions in the INGREDIENT PREPARATION scenario (we call this the RESULTANT STATE), as is further supported by these examples:

(5) *Bake* rolls 10 to 12 minutes or *until golden*.

(6) *Whirl* soup in batches in a blender *until very smooth*, pouring as blended into a bowl.

(7) In glass measuring cup, microwave milk on High 2 minutes or until warm.

Note that most of the items in the ADJ-slot express physical features which are perceivable to our olfactory, visual, and tactile senses.

Covarying collexeme analysis

The following table provides an overview of the top fifty of co-attraction patterns in lexemes that appear in the two slots:

Table 5: Top 50 covarying collexemes in [V *until* ADJ] (log-likelihood)

Rank	V	ADJ	CollStrength
1	process	smooth	77.4883250053926
2	whisk	smooth	74.3081493119387
3	heat	hot	71.7345772456578
4	chill	ready	62.1620612323359
5	cut	crumbly	57.341948534496
6	bake	brown	54.4547827592036
7	puree	smooth	52.0719010329519
8	bake	golden	45.5595208552395
9	beat	creamy	45.4066658218417
10	refrigerate	ready	44.6294558208117
11	soften	spoonable	44.1175683192719
12	heat	shimmering	38.7750581515116
13	blend	smooth	31.373010761743
14	beat	fluffy	30.005860958968
15	boil	tender	26.3781687405439
16	saut	tender	22.4441801401549
17	freeze	firm	21.2860298499074
18	hold	dry	19.7010715037720
19	stir	smooth	19.3741974765725
20	beat	light	18.6464000101095
21	cook	crisp	17.9965958940964

22	nest	cool	17.3311930525460
23	rinse	cool	17.3311930525460
24	microwave	hot	16.1354126392781
25	cook	fragrant	16.0913791525369
26	expand	strong²	15.0573771115997
27	glaze	sticky	15.0573771115997
28	grow	big	15.0573771115997
29	immerse	cold	15.0573771115997
30	press	thin	15.0573771115997
31	pull	taut	15.0573771115997
32	saut	soft	14.6883625441334
33	whirl	smooth	13.5857789047454
34	whisk	foamy	12.6615289640042
35	heat	simmering	12.6434399156316
36	bake	bubbly	12.2656271072162
37	cook	golden	11.3569249819187
38	blanch	tender	11.3179612328613
39	reduce	syrupy	11.2382921018308
40	cook	translucent	11.1466684324635
41	freeze	hard	10.0533528762178
42	soften	easy	10.0533528762178
43	steam	firm-tender	10.0533528762178
44	simmer	thick	9.7875591200796
45	churn	thick	9.65064260520371
46	dry	dry	9.65064260520371
47	mix	spreadable	9.65064260520371
48	fry	brown	9.35039018453113
49	cook	crisp-tender	9.34540668410136
50	cook	tender	9.33427256723814

It immediately becomes evident that most of the co-attracted items reflect a type of causal relation in which the ADJ-slot describes the RESULTANT STATE, as a feature or attribute, of the action described by the item in a V-slot.

A closer look at the covariant pairs, even those in which the lexemes in isolation do not seem to express any natural or obvious relation of causality, reveals that the construction indeed seems to serve to set up such a relation:

(8) *Mix* together cheese, 2 tsp. milk, and basil with a wooden spoon *until spreadable.*

(9) Reduce heat to low and simmer until syrupy and reduced by half, 4 to 5 minutes.

(10) *Nest* pot in ice water *until cool.*

'Mix' is associated with a causal relation in which two or more separate elements are combined into one; this causal relation is further elaborated in (8), where the mixing of the ingredients additionally results in a new texture of the substance into which the ingredients are combined and prepared for the next action – namely, that of spreading. 'Simmer' typically refers to the SITUATION OF COOKING AT A STEADY LOW HEAT TEMPERATURE, and thus has more of a self-contained type of actionality to it, describing an event without a natural completion point as such, but, in (9), it expresses a causal-telic meaning, since the syrupy consistency is construed as following from the simmering. 'Nest' has some causality to its conventional meaning, expressing the situation of placing an entity inside a container. Describing a situation as involving nesting, the interlocutor construes the situation such that the nested entity undergoes a physical relocation. In (10), an additional causal relation is added: as a result of being nested in ice water, the pot undergoes a change of temperature, which suggests that a locative prepositional phrase is necessary for causal construal.

Symbolic structure
Taking into account the principles of semantic compatibility (Stefanowitsch and Gries 2005, 4) and the principle of semantic coherence (Stefanowitsch and Gries 2005, 11), the observations made above reveal much of the semantic, and symbolic, structure of the [V *until* ADJ]-construction. The attraction of lexical items to both schematic slots in the construction indicates that the major semantic structure of the construction is the INGREDIENT PREPARATION frame, and, in suggesting that the

V-element evokes this frame, we have also already addressed an aspect of the symbolic structure of the construction. The telicity of most of the V-items in the top thirty indicates that CHANGE OF STATE is an important semantic component of the construction. Thus, we can conclude about the V-slot that it expresses acts of INGREDIENT PREPARATION in which the INGREDIENT also undergoes CHANGE OF STATE.

The construction elaborates on the INGREDIENT PREPARATION scenario by specifying a resultant attribute of the ingredient, which adds a CHANGE OF STATE to the INGREDIENT as part of a larger causal chain of the entire frame:

COOK → ACT OF PREPARATION → INGREDIENT (INITIAL STATE → RESULTANT STATE)

This elaboration, while still schematic, captures the underlying causal relation between the act and the resultant state. With the expanded, or specified, INGREDIENT PREPARATION scenario in place, the symbolic structure of the construction can be laid out, with the V-element symbolically linking up with the ACT OF PREPARATION, while the ADJ-element and 'until' both link up with the RESULTANT STATE, effectively making the construction symbolically non-monadic (Bache 1997, 159-166). While the ADJ-element specifies the RESULTANT STATE, "until" construes it as the ENDPOINT of the ACT OF PREPARATION. The other frame-components are implicit in the construction itself, but may be expressed by co-textual features in usage-events. This symbolic structure has two consequences for V-items which do not express CHANGE OF STATE. Firstly, we can expect them to display low collostruction strengths. Secondly, we can also expect many of them to undergo **coercion** (de Swart 2003), adopting functions which are semantically more compatible with the construction, as in (8-10).

Having set up a usage-based account of the symbolic structure of the construction, we shall now turn to a number of contextual and co-textual association patterns relating primarily to its external properties.

Illocutionary values

The V-slot features imperative, declarative, and infinitive verbs:

(11) *Process* first 6 ingredients in a food processor *until smooth*.

(12) I *roasted* it *until slightly crunchy* on the outside and tender in the middle.

(13) Let *stand* on a wire rack 5 minutes or *until dry*.

A simple frequency analysis suggests a preference for imperative forms with imperatives (= IMP) accounting for 95% of the distribution of mood in the V-slot, while declaratives (= DECL) and infinitives (= INF) account for 4% and 1% respectively:

Table 6: Distribution of mood in V-slot

IMP	DECL	INF
95% (n=652)	4% (n=24)	1% (n=9)

The imperative is often used in directive and instructive speech acts, and, logically, imperatives can be expected to generally be frequent in recipes. Indeed, Cotter (1997, 56) writes that "[t]he imperative verb forms are the recipe's most distinguishing syntactic feature and create internal cohesion between and among the discourse elements". The preference for imperative V-elements may be interpreted as another example of the conventions of the recipe genre percolating into the [V *until* ADJ]-construction.

The declarative realizations of the V-elements, specifically present participial ones, tend to appear in adverbial clauses that are attached to imperative main clauses:

(14) Add sugar, vanilla and egg, *blending until smooth*.

The construction serves as an adverbial in a simultaneity-expressing **cross-event relating structure** (Talmy 2000, 345) where the situation described in the adverbial clause takes place simultaneously with the situation described in the imperative main clause. That is, the adverbial clause instructs the reader to perform the act simultaneously with the act in the imperative main clause.[4]

This preference for imperatives may reflect illocutionary association patterns in instances of the construction. The distribution of illocutionary functions of the utterances containing the construction, unsurprisingly, shows a very clear preference for instructive speech acts over informative speech acts:

Table 7: Distribution of illocutionary functions

INSTRUCTIVES	INFORMATIVES
99% (n=679)	1% (n=6)

Below is an example of the construction used in a non-instructional text, this having an informative speech act function:

(15) We asked them to take away the wine bottle to free up space, and still it was difficult to reach for the wineglasses and take a sip. When the plates were removed, we could see a thick film of spattered broth and foie gras all over the glasses.

The dish itself was long on flash, short on substance. The breast was *cooked* sous vide style *until rare*, so a few swishes in the hot broth, fortified with a few slices of foie gras, heated and cooked it. It was the best part of the dish. Fat mushrooms and the thick-stemmed bok choy needed

more liquid than was provided by the nearly flat-surfaced pot, so they had to be eaten nearly raw. The broth was subtle and the two dipping sauces had sweet undercurrents, so I went for the wedge of lime and a little salt.

---

4   Like the declarative instances, the infinitive instances appear in imperative contexts themselves, as they are accompanied by imperative realizations of the catenative LET-construction as in 'Let stand until creamy' or 'Let sit until cool.'

In this particular case, the construction appears in a customer's description of eating in a restaurant, and, rather than being an instruction, [V until ADJ] describes how the dish was cooked. This shows that speakers do use the construction serving other communicative purposes than instructive ones, but, since this only accounts for 1% of the uses of the construction, we can take that as an indicator that the informative use of this construction is not a standard use.

Transitivity
The construction appears in three types of transitivity contexts. In the following examples, it appears with a direct object:

(16) *Chill* stuffing *until completely cool.*

(17) *In a medium nonstick skillet over medium heat, cook* onion and 4 garlic cloves *with remaining oil until golden, about 8 minutes.*

(18) *Meanwhile, beat cream cheese and granulated sugar with an electric mixer until smooth.*

Perhaps not surprisingly, the direct objects express the INGREDIENT in the INGREDIENT PREPARATION frame. In the following examples, the construction appears in passive contexts, in which the INGREDIENT is promoted to subject status:

(19) *At that point it* was covered and cooked *until tender.*

(20) *1 tablespoon tahini,* stirred *until homogenous.*

(21) *Any type of kale will work in this pasta sauce as long as it is wilted until tender before blending.*

Cases like (20) are considered reduced passives, since they have the same function as passive relative subclauses. The third transitivity context is that of the null-object (Culy 1996; Bender 1999; Massam and Roberge 1989), as seen in the following examples:

(22) *Bake* 22 minutes or *until golden brown* on top and bubbling.

(23) Cover and *cook* 10 minutes or *until very tender*, stirring occasionally.

(24) *Stir until smooth.*

Although it might be tempting to classify such cases as intransitive clauses, (22-24) still express two-participant scenarios in which an AGENT acts upon a formally unexpressed PATIENT.

A simple frequency analysis, seen in Table 8 below, shows that passive contexts are not very frequent, making up only 2% of the distribution of transitivity contexts, while monotransitive ones (= D-OBJ) account for 35%, and null-object contexts (= Ø-OBJ) account for no less than 63%:

Table 8: Distribution of transitivity contexts

D-OBJ	PASSIVE	Ø-OBJ
35% (n=241)	2% (n=12)	63% (n=432)

Why are null-object contexts more frequent with a construction that expresses two-participant situations than overtly monotransitive contexts are? Looking at larger co-textual chunks in the corpus may provide us with an answer. The construction appears most frequently, in the corpus, in texts of the type exemplified below:

(25) 1. Arrange a tight layer of malted milk balls (3 cups) over crust. *Stir* ice cream with cocoa powder and malted milk powder *until smooth*. Spoon into crust, set on a plate, and freeze 5 hours.
2. *Heat* 1/2 cup cream meanwhile *until simmering*. Put chocolate in a small metal bowl, pour in cream, and let sit until chocolate is melted, about 2 minutes. *Stir until smooth*. Let cool completely.
3. Smooth chocolate ganache over top of pie and *freeze until set*, about 15 minutes.
4. Whip remaining ½ cup cream and swirl onto pie. Chop some malted milk balls and drop onto pie; add a few whole balls. Remove rim and serve immediately.

This text is characterized by formal reduction, containing both determiner-less definite noun phrases and null-objects. These types of reduction constitute a feature of the text genre – namely, the recipe – that the construction typically occurs in (Culy 1996; Bender 1999; Massam and Roberge 1989). The genre is characterized by a register that observes formal economy with an emphasis on brief and succinct instructions, perhaps because the reader of a recipe often reads it while preparing the dish described in the recipe. Once a concept is discursively activated, recipes only make minimal overt reference to it, taking for granted that the reader has access to the concept and needs no further cuing in this respect. Consider (26), for instance, which reproduces some of the first instruction in (25) above:

(26) Stir ice cream with cocoa powder and malted milk powder until smooth. Spoon into crust, set on a plate, and freeze 5 hours.

The first sentence includes references to ice cream, cocoa powder and malted milk powder, describing how they are stirred together until they are turned into a smooth mass. The following sentence features no less than three null-object clauses. Still, it should be fairly obvious to the reader that the underlying, unexpressed, patient in these clauses corresponds to the resultant smooth blend of the three ingredients. Null-objects in English recipes have received some attention from linguists who generally agree that null-objects are typical features of the register of the recipe genre (Culy 1996; Bender 1999; Massam and Roberge 1989). For instance, Massam and Roberge (1989, 134) point out that, while null-objects are not common in English, they are nonetheless "found in certain discourse contexts, such as in recipes or other set of instructions". Thus, null-objects and other reduced forms appear to be stylistic features of the recipe genre, and thus conventional structures within the register associated with this genre. What happens in a case like (25-26) is probably that the [V *until* ADJ]-construction simply conforms to the conventions and communicative purpose of the recipe genre and its register, which is why the occurrence of the construction in null-object contexts is relatively high.

The reduced passives are probably infrequent because they describe actions, not as overt instructions, but rather as declaratives. In reality, however, the example in (20) is an indirect speech act, instructing the reader to perform the stirring before adding a spoonful of tahini. This is a communicatively disadvantageous way of presenting readers who are engaged in cooking while reading the recipe. As Cotter (1997, 62) writes, "preparing a dish is in effect moving through event space, the frame in which an event occurs [and e]ach action is predicated on what precedes and follows it." Failing to follow the temporal order of preparing a dish in a recipe might lead to misunderstandings, as Cotter (1997, 62) points out. In the light of Cotter's observation, the low frequency of [V *until* ADJ] in passive contexts can also be ascribed to the construction following the conventions of the language of recipes in English.

Temporality
The following examples show the construction occurring with time adverbials:

(27) Spread the potatoes on a nonstick baking sheet and *cook until slightly brown* and crispy, 30 to 40 minutes.

(28) Broil croquettes on oiled baking sheet 6" from heat, *turning until golden brown*, about 5 minutes.

(29) *Grill* vegetables 10 minutes or *until tender*, turning occasionally.

Here are examples of the construction appearing without time adverbials:

(30) *Blend* mixture in batches in blender or food processor *until very smooth*.

(31) When ready for dinner, *microwave* them *until hot* before adding to pasta.

(32) Add oil in a slow, steady stream, *whisking* constantly *until smooth*.

The distribution of temporal specifications does not as such indicate any specific affinity between the construction and temporal adverbials (= +TIME) or a lack thereof (=-TIME):

Table 9: Distribution of temporal contexts

-TIME	+TIME
44% (n=300)	56% (n=385)

What is interesting is that none of the +TIME contexts offer exact specifications of temporal extents as is clear in (27-28). This lack of temporal exactness indicates that the construction serves to set up a boundary of the temporal extent of the act of INGREDIENT PREPARATION, which is likely to be more reliable than time specifications. Thus the ADJ-element, by specifying the desired physical RESULTANT STATE of the INGREDIENT, provides the reader with a perceivable sensory cue as to the act's endpoint. This applies even to the unhedged time adverbials like in (29), because they are presented merely as alternatives to the desired state expressed by the ADJ-elements. The ADJ-element is thus an instance of what Cotter (1997) calls an **evaluative function**, providing an evaluative description of an element in the recipe, which requires that the reader makes use of his or her encyclopedic knowledge of cooking, and, if the reader lacks knowledge, he or she can use the time frame provided by temporal adverbials (in those cases that include time adverbials, that is).

Concluding remarks

The present corpus-based analysis of [V *until* ADJ] is, of course, not an exhaustive account of the construction. However, by investigating association patterns, we are able to account for a number of communicative functions, which would not even be possible in an account based on Chomsky's view of competence.

The collostructional analyses helped us identify the semantic structure and, thus, the symbolic structure of the construction, as the patterns of attraction of lexemes to the two schematic slots indicate that the construction is used primarily to express an INGREDIENT PREPARATION frame in which an INGREDIENT is being treated such that it undergoes a CHANGE OF STATE. The attraction of verbs that belong to cookery terminology to the V-slot further indicates that the construction is closely associated with the register of cookery. This is further supported by the frequent occurrence of the construction in null-object contexts, which is itself a typical trait of the recipe genre, and, of course, by the fact that the construction appears most frequently in recipes in which it serves primarily instructive illocutionary functions, as illustrated by the preference for imperative verbs in the V-slot. These association patterns indicate that the construction's primary communicative function is to instruct readers in how to prepare ingredients when cooking and that the construction itself is conventionally associated with the register of the genre of recipes. Moreover, the distribution of temporal markers in the immediate co-text – covering either an absence of temporal markers or temporal markers which are not exact – further suggests, in conjunction with the attraction of items to the ADJ-slot that express perceivable physical states, that the construction serves to provide the reader with a physical cue as to when the ingredient preparation is complete, and that this cue takes priority over exact temporal specifications.

Our analysis accounts for some very specific external features of the construction, which are integral to our understanding of how the construction is used. It is only logical to assume that speakers know when and how to use the construction, and which communicative purposes it serves. In other words, these external properties form vital aspects of the knowledge, or competence, associated with the construction. Had we adopted the Chomskian version of competence, in which performance is a degenerated version of competence, we would never have been able to provide a communicatively relevant description of [V *until* ADJ]. However, as we have seen, a usage-based perspective in which there is a mutual interplay between performance and competence, allows us to do so, because it justifies the empirical study of language use and makes valid naturally occurring linguistic data in the building of models of the language system and, thus, of language competence.

References

Bache, Carl. 1997. *The Study of Aspect, Tense and Action: Towards a Theory of the Semantics of Grammatical Categories*, 2nd ed. Frankfurt am Main: Peter Lang.

Bender, Emily. 1999. "Constituting context: Null objects in English recipes revisited". *U. Penn Working Papers in Linguistics*, 6(1): 53-68.

Bergen, Benjamin K., and Nancy C. Chang. 2005. "Embodied construction grammar in simulation-based language understanding". In *Construction Grammar(s): Cognitive and Cross-language Dimensions*, edited by Jan-Ola Östman and Mirjam Fried, 145-190. Amsterdam: John Benjamins.

Biber, Douglas, Susan Conrad, and Randi Reppen. 1998. *Corpus Linguistics: Investigating Language Structure and Use*. Cambridge: Cambridge University Press.

Bybee, Joan and Paul J. Hopper. 2001. "Introduction to frequency and the emergence of linguistic structure". In *Frequency and the Emergence of Linguistic Structure*, edited by Joan Bybee and Paul Hopper, 1-24. Amsterdam: John Benjamins.

Chomsky, Noam. 1965. *Aspects of the Theory of Syntax*. Cambridge, MA: MIT Press.

Cotter, Colleen. 1997. "Claiming a piece of the pie: How the language of recipes defines community". In *Recipes for Reading: Community Cookbooks, Stories, Histories*, edited by Anne L. Bower, 51-72. Amherst, MA: University of Massachusetts Press.

Croft, William A. 2001. *Radical Construction Grammar: Syntactic Theory in Typological Perspective*. Oxford: Oxford University Press.

Croft, William A. 2003. "Lexical rules vs. constructions: A false dichotomy". In *Motivation in Language: Studies in Honour of Günter Radden*, edited by Hubert Cuyckens, Thomas Berg, René Dirven and Klaus-Uwe Panther, 49-68. Amsterdam: John Benjamins.

Croft, William A. 2005. "Logical and typological arguments for Radical Construction Grammar". In *Construction Grammars: Cognitive Grounding and Theoretical Extensions*, edited by Jan-Ola Östman, 273-314. Amsterdam: John Benjamins.

Croft, William A., and D.A. Cruse. 2004. *Cognitive Linguistics*. Cambridge: Cambridge University Press.

Culy, Christopher. 1996. "Null objects in English recipes". *Language Variation and Change* 8(1): 91-124.

Davies, Mark. 2012. *Corpus of Contemporary American English*. http://corpus2.byu.edu/coca (accessed November 14, 2012)

Dunning, Ted. 1993. "Accurate methods for the statistics of surprise and coincidence". *Computational Linguistics*, 19(1): 61–74.

Fillmore, Charles J. 1982. "Frame semantics". In *Linguistics in the Morning Calm*, edited by The Linguistic Society of Korea, 111-137. Seoul: Hanshin.

Fillmore, Charles J. 1988. "The mechanisms of "Construction Grammar"". In *Proceedings of the Fourteenth Annual Meeting of the Berkeley Linguistics Society*, edited by Annie Jaisser, Shelley Axmaker, and Helen Singmaster, 35-55. Berkeley, CA: Berkeley Linguistics Society.

Fillmore, Charles J., Paul Kay, and Mary Catherine O'Connor. 1988. "Regularity and idiomaticity in grammatical constructions: The case of *let alone*. *Language*, 64(3): 501-539.

Goldberg, Adele E. 1995. *Constructions: A Construction Grammar Approach to Argument Structure*. Chicago: Chicago University Press.

Gries, Stefan Th. 2007. *Coll.analysis 3.2a: A Program for R for Windows 2.x.*

Hopper, Paul J. 1998. "Emergent grammar". In *The New Psychology of Language: Cognitive and Functional Approaches to Language Structure*, edited by Michael Tomasello, 155-175. Mahwah, NJ: Lawrence Erlbaum.

Hymes, Dell. 1972. *Towards Communicative Competence*. Philadelphia; PA: University of Pennsylvania Press.

Jensen, Kim Ebensgaard. 2012. "Fatal attraction: Inheritance and collostruction in the ihjel-construction". *Skandinaviske Sprogstudier* 3(2): 1-30.

Kemmer, Suzanne, and Michael Barlow. 2000. "Introduction: A usage-based conception of language". In *Usage-Based Models of Language*, edited by Michael Barlow and Suzanne Kemmer, vii-xxviii. Stanford, CA: Stanford University Press.

Langacker, Ronald W. 1987. *Foundations of Cognitive Grammar – Vol. 1: Theoretical Prerequisites*. Stanford, CA: Stanford University Press.

Massam, Diane, and Yves Roberge. 1989. "Recipe context null objects in English". *Linguistic Inquiry* 20 (1): 134-139.

Pedersen, Ted. 1996. "Fishing for exactness". *Proceedings of the SCSUG 96 in Austin, TX*, 188-200.

de Saussure, Ferdinand. 1983 [1916]. *Course in General Linguistics*. Translated by Roy Harris. London: Duckworth.

Stefanowitsch, Anatol and Stefan Th. Gries. 2003. "Collostructions: Investigating the interaction between words and constructions". *International Journal of Corpus Linguistics* 8(2): 2-43.

Stefanowitsch, Anatol and Stefan Th. Gries. 2005. "Covarying collexemes". *Corpus Linguistics and Linguistic Theory* 1(1): 1-43.

de Swart, Henrietta. 2003. "Coercion in a cross-linguistic theory of aspect". In *Mismatch: Form-Function Incongruity and the Architecture of Grammar*, edited by Elaine J. Francis and Laura A. Michaelis, 231-258. Stanford, CA: Stanford University Press.

Talmy, Leonard. 2000. *Toward a Cognitive Semantics – vol. 1: Concept Structuring Systems*. Cambridge, MA: MIT Press.

Tomasello, Michael. 2003. *Constructing a Language: A Usage-Based Theory of Language Acquisition*. Cambridge, MA: Havard University Press.

Linguistic Competences:
Do they really need improving?

Anna Kristina Hultgren

Abstract
In today's globalized societies, characterized by increased translingual, multimodal and sometimes fast-paced communication, the concept "linguistic competences" has become a highly prolific notion. It is frequently invoked as the remedy for all sorts of problems, and lack thereof is seen as the root of all evils (Cameron 2000a). This paper offers a critical sociolinguistic approach to the notion of linguistic competences. It asks what people actually mean by "linguistic competences" and why it has apparently become such a central concept in contemporary society. Drawing on examples from two contexts, the globalized call centre industry and the eight internationalized universities of Denmark, the paper first examines the meaning of linguistic competences. Here, it finds that a strengthening of linguistic competences is hailed as the same solution to problems which are very different in nature and which are perceived to exist in both the call centres and the universities. Drawing on Cameron's notion of "verbal hygiene" (2012a), it then proposes that the preoccupation with language, and more specifically with linguistic competences, may be interpreted as a symbolic act for a much more fundamental urge of human being to put the world to right. In this interpretation, inter-

ventions in the social order come to be conflated with interventions in language, and more specifically in linguistic competences.

Introduction: "linguistic competences" as a pseudo-problem?

> Every community in Europe can become more language-friendly by making better use of opportunities to hear and see other languages and cultures, thereby helping to improve language awareness and learning (European Commission 2003: 12)

As this excerpt from a European Commission whitepaper epitomizes, competences in other languages have come to be seen as highly important in the globalized world. Part of the explanation for this may be that the world has become increasingly translingual, transcultural and transnational which arguably puts extra pressure on making oneself understood. Thus, there is some logic to the argument that the development of linguistic competences is more important today than it has been at other points in history where communication, both face-to-face and virtual, between speakers of different languages was perhaps not as intense and widespread as it is today.

Nevertheless, this paper approaches the notion of "linguistic competences" from a critical angle. It asks what people actually mean by "linguistic competences" and why it is so frequently invoked as a crucial concept in contemporary society. It raises the question of whether it is always appropriate or helpful to accord linguistic competence with the attention that it apparently attracts, drawing on examples from two types of workplaces in which linguistic competences are hailed as the solution to potential problems of various kinds, the globalized call centre industry and the eight internationalized universities of Denmark. Customers dealing with call centres often complain about a variety of non-linguistic problems: long waiting times, being transferred between different departments, not getting an adequate solution to their query, etc., yet it is rarely the case that the organizational and systemic factors which cause such problems are addressed. Instead, what receives attention in call centres are the call centre agents' communication skills, which are subject to intense scrutiny by the management (Cameron 2000b, Taylor et al. 2002, Hultgren 2011). Similarly, universities in Denmark and elsewhere are undergoing significant structural changes centred on internationalization, competition and marketization (Altbach and Knight 2007, Hazelkorn 2011, Hultgren 2013). In non-English dominant countries, this tends to lead to Englishization, i.e. an increased use of English in teaching, research publication and administration (Hultgren 2013). In the Danish and Nordic contexts, one solution which has been proposed to curb these developments is the introduction of parallellingual language policies, i.e. a strengthening of the linguistic or communicative competences in English, Danish and other languages among staff and students (Hultgren 2014).

The paper draws on data in the form of institutional documents in call centres and universities which hail linguistic competences as being in need of attention (Hultgren 2011, 2014). In call centres, such linguistic competences are typically referred to as "communication skills", where in universities, they may be referred to variously as "linguistic competences" [sproglige kompetencer] or "communicative competences". My data from call centres includes communication training material, customer service manuals and scorecards used in staff performance reviews collected from call centres in the Philippines, Hong Kong, Denmark and Scotland. In universities, it takes the form of language policy documents devised by each of Denmark's eight universities. On the basis of these sets of documents, I aim to show that linguistic competences (in some form) is presented as a key notion and often in need of improvement. I shall then go on to question, whether the culprit is indeed insufficient linguistic competences, or whether something else might be at stake.

Despite the fact that universities and call centres might immediately strike us as being quite different: one is high status and part of the knowledge economy and the other comparatively low status and part of the service economy, they also have one thing in common, which is the way in which the management stipulates certain guidelines as to their employees' linguistic and communicative competences. Partly, this concern must be seen in light of the communicative activities in both these types of institution often taking place between language users with different first languages (Haberland et al. 2013, Duchêne 2009) and of universities and call centres both being profoundly affected by globalizing and/or internationalizing processes (Altbach and Knight 2007, Hazelkorn 2011, Hultgren 2013, Heller 2003, Taylor et al. 2002, Hultgren 2011). As far as call centres are concerned, it is useful to draw a distinction between on- and offshore call centres. Onshore are those which are based in the same country as the organization of which they are a part and in which agents and customers share the same first language. Offshore call centres, by contrast, are those outsourced overseas, and in which agents often communicate with customers in a language which is not their first, e.g. English as a second language users in Indian or Philippine call centres communicating with customers in the UK and the United States. Whilst it is perhaps to be expected that offshore call centres are concerned with language competences, given that the employees almost exclusively undertake all job functions in a language which is not their first, as we shall see in this paper, language competences, or communication skills, is also a highly salient notion in onshore call centres. Similarly, just as the way of organizing service work has changed dramatically as a consequence of technological advances and the removal of cross-national trade barriers, universities across Europe are undergoing similar changes centred on internationalization, competition and marketization, which bring them more into line with one another and, more similar to a corporation than a public institution (Fairclough 1993). In universities in non-English-dominant countries, this has led to an increased use of English in teaching, research and administration, Englishization, and, consequently, an increased concern with strengthening linguistic competences (Altbach and Knight 2007, Hazelkorn 2011, Hultgren 2013). Thus, globalizing processes centred on neo-liberalism have transformed institutions in the service and knowledge sector alike and, for reasons which shall be scrutinized in this paper, placed linguistic competences at centre stage.

Linguistic competences: Theoretical approach
In this section, I outline the theoretical approach, rooted in socio- and applied linguistics, to linguistic competences adopted in this paper. I begin with a brief outline of some recent theoretical developments before I proceed to outlining the theory of verbal hygiene (Cameron 2012a).

Linguistic competences: from system to practice
Recent developments in socio- and applied linguistics have seen a move away from viewing language as a system which exists a priori of discourse to seeing it instead as something that cannot and should not be detached from usage (Jørgensen 2008, Møller 2008, García 2009, Creese and Blackledge 2010, Otsuji and Pennycook 2010, Jaspers 2011). Evidence to support this argument is drawn from bi- or multilingually competent speakers who comfortably switch in and out of different "languages" – in the common-sense definition of referring to delimitable entities such as "English", "Punjabi", "Swahili", etc. – often without even realizing that they do so. New terms, such as poly- and translanguaging, metro- and zerolingualism have been proposed to highlight the need for such a reconceptualization (Møller 2008, García 2009, Creese and Blackledge 2010, Otsuji and Pennycook 2010, Jaspers 2011).

If we accept the view that *language as a system* is played down – by language users and language analysts alike – in favour of *communicative practice*, then this has significant consequences for how we conceptualize linguistic competences. If there is no system to refer back to, then how can it be determined what is correct and incorrect, competent or incompetent? This is in fact a point which has been argued quite strongly in relation to non-native users of English by English as a Lingua Franca (ELF) scholars who propose that because those who use English as a second or foreign language now outnumber native speakers by far, it makes no sense for learners of English to have their competence judged by native-speaker criteria (Seidlhofer 2011, Jenkins et al. 2011, Dewey 2012). Instead, it is argued, we need to shift attention away from a system to a communicative understanding of linguistic competence. Instead of asking: "Do English language learners remember to add an "s" to their verbs in the third person singular?", we need to ask: "Do they manage to get their point across?". Similarly, Canagarajah argues that (English) language teaching needs to move away from teaching discrete items, such as grammar, phonetics and lexis to teaching speakers to negotiate meaning and communicate pragmatically via a repertoire of linguistic resources such as code-switching, accommodation, interpersonal skills and attitudinal stances (Canagarajah 2007).

Such attempts at reconceptualizing linguistic competence, here manifested as English language competence specifically, have not escaped criticism. It has been argued that adopting ELF as a pedagogical principle might be doing students a disfavour. Taylor, e.g, suggests that we should not assume a priori that students who prefer to strive for "a near-native variety" constitute a minority in the world (Taylor 2006: 52). Others point out that, despite claims to the contrary, it is not clear how ELF would be fairer than more "established" (and I use this word advisedly) ways of speaking English, and that disadvantages faced by non-native users of English are likely to persist in spite of renaming "English" to "English as a Lingua Franca" (Gazzola and Grin 2013). Others have questioned the relevance of ELF findings to higher education where "accuracy of lexis, syntax, and discourse in both speech and writing, and international intelligibility, are of paramount importance" (Phillipson 2015). What might be particularly clear from such debates about the form and relevance of linguistic competence is the sociolinguistic principle that language norms are not set in stone, but are under continuous negotiation. It has been suggested that in times of intensified physical and virtual contact between language users, a hallmark of our contemporary globalized society, it is particularly common for linguistic norms to be overtly negotiated and actively reflected upon (Makihara and Shieffelin 2007, Duchêne and Heller 2008, Cameron 2012a).

Linguistic competences and "verbal hygiene"
This insight leads us nicely onto the notion of "verbal hygiene" developed by the British sociolinguist Deborah Cameron (Cameron 2012a[1995]). The central tenet of "verbal hygiene" is that any preoccupation with language (and, by extension, linguistic competences) may be interpreted as being in essence about something else. In what follows, this argument is laid out in greater detail.

In an online article aimed at the general public, Cameron (2013) illustrates her point with a topical example from the United Kingdom: In recent years, British politicians have become increasingly obsessed with English-language competences, and particularly with the need for immigrants to develop such skills. It has become commonplace, she notes, to "bang[...] on about the importance of English, and the menace of the immigrant who can't/won't speak it". As evidence of this obsession, Cameron points to the fact that, for the first time ever, the 2011 census, which is a form to be filled out by every household in Britain, asked respondents to tick how well they spoke English. Cameron argues, that British politicians' obsession with migrants' "refusal" to learn English is making "a mountain out of a mole-hill". While, on the one hand, the media are headlining stories such as "Polish now Britain's second language" and "22% of households in London contain no one who has English as their main language", the census data itself, provides us with the insight that only a very slight minority of the British population do not speak any English at all. 1.6% of the population declare that they have limited or no proficiency in English, whereas those with no proficiency constitute less than 0.5%. As Cameron points out, these 0.5% may well contain both pre-school-aged children and people who have just arrived in Britain.

According to Cameron, the tendency in contemporary society to make "a mountain out of a mole-hill" as far as language competences are concerned was prompted by two major events: on the one hand, increasing popular concern about rising numbers of immigrants, and, on the other, increasing anxiety about the threat of radical Islam. The latter was seen not only as an external threat, but also as an internal one, especially after the "7/7" bombings that killed more than 50 people in London in July 2005. Cameron argues that these events have caused British politicians to view English-language competences as a symbol of civilized Britishness. Cameron writes: "All the mainstream political parties now deploy a kind of rhetoric in which speaking English is a patriotic duty, while not speaking it is a threat to national unity and 'social cohesion'". This rhetoric is not dissimilar to that which has circulated in Denmark surrounding both the integration of immigrants and the Englishization of Danish universities (Jørgensen and Holmen 2010). Regarding the former, the main party of the current coalition government, the Social Democrats, have proposed introducing a so-called "Integrationspålæg" [integration mandate] (Danish Parliament 2013). This is intended to make immigrants' receipt of social benefits contingent upon them learning Danish. As Cameron points out, however, with regard to the British context, the purported link between not speaking English and being alienated from British society is inconveniently contradicted by the fact that the men who carried out the 7/7 terrorist attacks were born and bred in Britain and left their suicide videos in fluent, Yorkshire-accented, English. In this case, then, Cameron argues, "language becomes a metaphor for the clash of civilizations" (2012b). She explains:

> In any given time and place, the most salient forms of verbal hygiene will tend to be linked to other preoccupations which are not primarily linguistic, but are rather social, political and moral. The logic behind verbal hygiene depends on a common-sense analogy between the order of language and the larger social order, or the order of the world. The rules of language stand in for the rules that govern social or moral conduct and putting language to right becomes a sort of symbolic surrogate for putting the world to right (Cameron 2012b: transcribed from an oral presentation).

If a preoccupation with language and linguistic competences really is a cover preoccupation for some deeper anxieties about the world, then, as Cameron suggests, this would explain why opinions about language are often expressed with such passion and fervour. Because, as she says, in most cases they are "not just debates about language" (Cameron 2012b), but debates about the current state of the world and about how to put it right. Below, we shall have a closer look at two institutional contexts, call centres and universities, in which linguistic and communicative competences are similarly construed as being in need of improvement with seemingly little consideration for the possibility that this might not always be the most relevant response.

Linguistic competences in the globalized call centre industry

In this section, we will have a look at what constitutes "communication skills" in the globalized call centre industry. Linguistic competences in the globalized call centre industry are in high demand.[1] This is the case whether or not the call centre is on- or offshore. In one of my research sites, an offshore call centre in the Philippines, in which agents communicated with customers located in the US, agents had to take courses in English as a second language, although their English proficiency was already high, since only 4% of applicants to this call centre were deemed to have sufficiently high competences in English to get a job. Once hired, they had to follow extensive training programmes which focused on particular aspects of the customer service interaction which might pose particular problems, such as how to pronounce US place names or surnames correctly, place the stress in the right place, use appropriate address terms, and so on. It also gave them training in grammar, e.g. how and when to use modals appropriately, and a range of other aspects (Hultgren 2011). Indian call centre agents have been found to have to take courses to "neutralize" their Indian accent on the presumption that this will make them "more intelligible" to Western-based customers who may not have had sufficient exposure to the access to be familiar with it (Cowie 2007). Typically, agents in offshore call centres also receive culture training, which may consist of watching British or American soaps to enable them to engage in small talk – seen as crucial for rapport-building purposes – with customers about last night's episode. As is well-known, many offshore call centres also give their agents English-sounding names in an attempt to conceal the location of the call centre, knowing that offshore call centres have a particularly bad reputation. In the onshore Hong Kong call centre I researched, agents were, despite the fact that they dealt only with domestic clients, specifically recruited for their trilingual skills because these enabled them to answer calls from all three customer groups: Cantonese-speaking (the vast majority), English-speaking (expats living in Hong Kong, typically constituting 5% of customers) and Mandarin-speaking (typically 1-2% of customers). Research from Canadian call centres has found that

---

1   Most organizations today, whether in the private or public sector, make use of specially dedicated call centres to take care of their contact with customers. Call centres can be both in- and outbound. Inbound call centres are those where they majority of calls are customer-initiated and typically relate to account inquiries. In outbound call centres, the majority of calls are to the customers, and they are often unsolicited (known as cold calls) typically with the purpose of trying to sell something.

English-French bilinguals are also in high demand for their potential to communicate with more than one type of customers (Heller 2003).

However, aside from the obvious necessity of agents dealing with customers with another L1 than themselves having linguistic competences, there is more to it than that. Linguistic competences in call centres are as much about rapport-building and politeness as they are about grammatically correct standard British or American English. This is probably the reason why the phenomenon with which we are concerned here is construed as "communication skills" rather than "linguistic competences". This becomes particularly clear when we turn our attention more specifically to the two call centres in Denmark and Scotland, in which I conducted research, and in which agents communicate in their first language with customers based in the same country. Here too, there was a considerable focus on communication skills and extensive resources were committed to teaching them. Agents in these call centres underwent an almost equally strict communication training programme as in the offshore call centres. They received training in how to create rapport, how to greet the customer, how to engage them in small talk, how to ask questions appropriately, both to control the call, but also to elicit the appropriate information from the customer, how to signal that they were listening to the customer, how to terminate a call in the best way, which words to use and which to avoid, and how to show empathy and understanding. The only difference from the offshore call centre was that agents did not receive training in grammar or phonetics since they were speaking to customers in their first language. What is taught in the training sessions is typically also encoded in customer service manuals and/or interaction prompts, which the agents must typically refer to in any interaction. The adherence to these prescriptions is strictly monitored in regular assessment sessions, the outcome of which is potentially consequential for promotion. All in all, then, there is hardly any doubt that communication skills in call centres are hugely important.

Analysed as an instance of "verbal hygiene", it could be argued that the extreme focus on communication skills in call centres is a pseudo-solution. While it might be conceded that being polite, courteous and understanding has both social and economic benefits measured in terms of returning customers, it is unlikely to solve many of the more systemic problems of call centres. The organizational setup of call centres is such that it enables a maximum number of customers to be dealt with in as short time as possible (Cameron 2000b, Taylor et al. 2002, Hultgren 2011). Call centres agents are often trained to deal only with specific types of queries, which is why, as a customer, you may have to press a specific key to ensure that you are put through to the right person. Targets often exist for how many calls must be taken in a specific time period, and employees may be actively encouraged to shorten their calls (Hultgren 2011). Such deliberately hyper-rationalized institutions may create problems for customers, who may be transferred between various departments before being put through to a person authorized to deal with their request or who may not have their query resolved because of the rigidity of the system. Yet, the instinct in call centres is to resort to a superficial intervention of improving the call centre agents' communication skills, since altering the organizational structure would undermine the entire raison d'être of call centres. Put in another way, instead of trying to eradicate the actual causes of customers' problems, call centres train agents to apologize politely for when it inevitably does go wrong.

Linguistic competences in the internationalized universities
At Denmark's universities, linguistic competences have for some time now been seen as in need of attention. In a recent article, I examine the language policies of Denmark's eight universities (it is in itself interesting that the universities all *have* language policies) and I find that all policies emphasize the importance of linguistic competences (Hultgren 2014). The excerpt shown below from the language policy of the University of Aalborg (2005) may serve as an illustration:

The purpose of the University of Aalborg's language policy is to contribute to raising the *communicative competence* [my emphasis] in research and teaching undertaken at the university by

1. Maintaining and developing the Danish language as a fundamental written and spoken language of research and teaching at the university and

2. Using English and, where necessary, other relevant foreign languages, where it is needed to retain and develop the University of Aalborg as an active partner and player in the global knowledge society.[2]

Part of the concern with "raising the communicative competence" might be interpreted as a genuine and constructive attempt at meeting the needs that arise in a changing workplace where employees of a range of different first-language background interact (Haberland et al. 2013). For example, some universities in Denmark have established support centres which provide, e.g., courses in Danish for international faculty, English for administrative staff, academic writing for faculty and research students and so on.

There is also an argument, however, that the concern with *communicative competences* and, more generally, language policy is a response to some underlying concerns which may or may not be solely or even primarily language-related. Universities in Denmark have, as European universities in general, undergone significant changes in the past one or two decades. As a result of various policies at EU, national and institutional level, there is now a much greater use of English in teaching, publications and internal communication than there has been before (Hultgren 2013). The Bologna Declaration, for example, ratified by Denmark in 1999, was an agreement aimed at standardizing European degree structures and promoting mobility to strengthen the European zone of higher education and research vis-à-vis the US. This led to more English-taught programmes at Danish universities (Phillipson 2006). Similarly, the introduction in 2010 of the bibliometric research indicator ("bibliometrisk forskningsindikator"), akin to the British Research Assessment Excercise

---

2   Translated by the author from the orginal Danish version: Sprogpolitikken for Aalborg Universitet har til formål at bidrage til højnelse af den kommunikative kompetence i universitetets forskning og undervisning ved
    1. At vedligeholde og udvikle det danske sprog som grundlæggende skrift- og talesprog for forskningen og undervisningen på universitetet og
    2. At anvende engelsk og evt. andre relevante fremmedsprog, hvor det er påkrævet for at fastholde og udvikle Aalborg Universitet som en aktiv partner og medspiller i det globale videnskabelige samfund.

and Research Excellence Framework, meant that Danish universities were allocated public funds according to the quality and quantity of their research output; the greater the number in high-ranking journals, the more money from the state. This too engenders a greater use of English since high-ranking journals are, with very few exceptions, English-medium (see also Gazzola 2012). At institutional level, universities often have targets to increase their intake of non-Danish research staff and students, which also contributes to a greater use of English (Saarinen and Nikula 2013).

The concerns which have been voiced over such Englishization have led to all Danish universities having some sort of language policy, whose overall purpose is typically to declare the institution officially bi- or multilingual. In some cases this is referred to as a parallellingual language policy, with reference to a recommendation from the Nordic Council (Nordic Council of Ministers 2007). The purpose of a parallellingual language policy is to ensure the continued use of Danish alongside English without the latter encroaching on the former. This dual (or "parallel") use of the national language Danish and international languages is echoed in the language policy of Aalborg University, which highlights the need to "maintain and develop the Danish language" on the one hand, and, on the other, to "retain and develop the University of Aalborg as an active partner and participant in the global knowledge society" by "[u]sing English and, where necessary, other relevant foreign languages, where it is needed". The concern with strengthening communicative competence thus relates both to English and to Danish. Let us consider each of these concerns in turn and examine the assumptions on which they are based.

Concerns about the future state of the Danish language have, over the past two decades or so, regularly been voiced (Haberland et al. 1991, Jarvad 2001, 2008, Danish Language Council 2003, 2007, Danish Ministry of Culture 2003, 2004, 2008, 2009; Kirchmeier-Andersen 2008, Harder 2009, Siiner 2010). One concern which has been expressed in relation to this is that graduates may not be able to communicate with practitioners and serve the Danish society if they have been trained in English only. Airey's (2009, 2015) research on undergraduate physics students in Sweden who received their training in both Swedish in English seems to contradict this. The majority of students he interviewed were able to explain physics concepts in both Swedish and English, irrespective of the language in which the concepts had been taught. Thus, on the basis of this data, it would appear that one cannot automatically assume that receiving one's training in one language will hinder successful communication about that topic in another. Concerns have also been raised about segments of Danish society who are not competent in English, which according to some estimates may constitute as much as 20% of the population (Preisler 1999), being prevented from accessing new knowledge when this has been produced in English. However, such concerns tend not to be substantiated by evidence, and they seem to overlook the fact that there is always a certain amount of "translation" going on from a specialized to a popularized text even when these are produced in the same language. Thus, it is not clear whether the gap between scientists and the wider society is larger now than it has been at other points in history, or if it is rather the case that Englishization has helped made visible gaps which have always existed.

As regards competences in English, concerns have been raised about the quality of teaching and learning being lowered when it is undertaken in English, a language that the majority of teachers and students do not have as their first language (Danish Ministry of Culture 2003, 2004, 2008, 2009; Kirchmeier-Andersen 2008, Harder 2009). Often, a strengthening of language or communicative competences in the case of Aalborg University's language policy, is advocated to prevent this from happening. However, the lack of clarity and precision about what *communicative competence* is taken to mean more specifically, prevents us from judging the relevance of invoking this concept. If what is thought of here is native-speaker competence at all levels of the linguistic system then presumably very few have adequate linguistic competences in English and it may well be questioned how relevant it would be for actors in this context to acquire such competences. Research by Klaasen (2001), e.g., conducted at a technical university in the Netherlands (a country which in terms of English-language competences is on a par with Scandinavia (EF 2011)), suggests that as long as a lecturer's level of English language competence is above a certain base level, type of pedagogy appears to be more important than language of instruction. Klaassen recorded lectures in Dutch and English and asked students to rate them according to comprehensibility and student-centrednes. She found that for lecturers whose TOEFL score was above 580 (equivalent of approximately C1[3] on the Common European Framework Council of Europe), the degree to which the lecturer adopted a student-centred pedagogy was more important the language competence. In a follow-up study which assessed the language competences of scientific staff at Delft University of Technology, Klaassen and Bos (2010) found that the majority of scientific staff (55%) actually had C1 level competence in English. While this does suggest a possible need for developing English-language competences among those lecturers whose proficiency is below the threshold, as well as, possibly for students, it also suggests that in the majority of cases it might be more helpful to address pedagogic methods than language competence.

The research undertaken so far on the relationship between English-language instruction and learning outcome seems to be inconclusive. On the one hand, most lecturers who do not have English as their L1 seem to report that their level of English is sufficient for them to be able to teach in English (Airey 2011, Jakobsen 2010, Jensen and Thøgersen 2011, Klaassen 2001, Vinke 1995), however they are also able to point to challenges, such as lack of nuance (both lexical and grammatical) and precision, reduced ability to draw on humour, storytelling and cultural examples to make connections in teaching, as well as increased workload (Airey 2011, Hellekjær 2007, Vinke 1995). Students too have been found to report more problems following a lecture in English than in their first language (e.g. Hellekjær 2010). Interestingly, a positive correlation has also been shown between students' perceptions of, on the one hand, how well a non-native-speaking English lecturer speaks Eng-

---

[3] Descriptive criteria for this level are:
 – Can understand a wide range of demanding, longer texts, and recognise implicit meaning.
 – Can express ideas fluently and spontaneously without much obvious searching for expressions.
 – Can use language flexibly and effectively for social, academic and professional purposes.
 – Can produce clear, well-structured, detailed text on complex subjects, showing controlled use of organisational patterns, connectors and cohesive devices (Council of Europe 2011).

lish and, on the other, their teaching abilities and subject knowledge (Jensen et al. 2013). Researchers who have compared a lecture delivered in Danish with one delivered in English by the same lecturer have also found evidence of a slower speech rate and a more formal delivery when teaching in English compared to teaching in Danish (Airey and Thøgersen 2011). Others have shown that students may ask fewer questions and have more difficulties taking notes when they are taught in English (Airey 2009, 2015). What remains unclear, however, is the extent to which such reported challenges and observed differences actually have a bearing on learning outcome as such, which is the argument on which a strengthening of language competences is based.

It has been found, e.g., that students compensate for any perceived difficulties by preparing better for the lessons or by asking questions *after* the lesson instead of during it (Airey 2009). Similarly, it is not clear if a slower and more formal delivery of interaction will necessarily lead to a lower learning uptake. Klaassen found that although there *is* evidence to suggest that there may be a steeper learning curve in English medium instruction, any initial difficulties are likely to disappear after a year (Klaassen 2001). Part of the reason why documenting a link between English-language competence and learning outcome has proved so difficult might have to do with learning being an immensely complex process, which depends on an infinite range of factors not all of which can be foreseen, let alone controlled for in any given study. All in all, then, on the balance of the evidence, it might be that the call for a strengthening of language or communicative competences is too imprecise and general to be particularly helpful or useful.

Conclusion
In this paper, I have argued that the focus on language competences, whether in the wider society, or in globalized/internationalized institutions such as call centres and universities, may be interpreted as an act of "verbal hygiene" (Cameron 2012a). This means that a preoccupation with language, and more specifically language competences (whether construed as "communication skills" as in call centres or "communicative competence" as in some universities) may be interpreted as an at-

tempt at putting to right things that are felt to be in disorder in the world in general. Such things might relate back to the many changes brought about by globalization, which has drastically changed the ways in which service provision and higher education is organized. Linguistic competences apparently come to be seen as the one thing about which something can actually be done, whether or not this is in fact the most effective remedy. This is of course not to deny the usefulness of developing language competences. Nor is it to deny the likelihood that service workers and university staff and students might benefit from better resources, more time, lower workload and a sharpened focus on their individual and collective needs to do the job they are asked to do. Rather, what I have tried to do here is to adopt a critical sociolinguistic approach to the notion of linguistic competence, and to suggest the possibility the attention accorded to it may be disproportionate to its relevance. It is worth considering the extent to which the obsession with linguistic competences obscures and detracts attention away from more fundamental neoliberal processes with undeniable effects on the ways in which service work and higher education and research are organized.

References

Airey, John. 2015. "From Stimulated Recall to Disciplinary Literacy: Summarizing Ten Years of Research into Teaching and Learning in English." In *English-medium Instruction at European Universities*, edited by Slobodanka Dimova, Anna Kristina Hultgren, and Christian Jensen. Berlin: Mouton, 2015.

Airey, John. 2011. "Talking about teaching in English: Swedish university lecturers? Experiences of changing teaching language." *Ibérica* 22:35–54.

Airey, John. 2009. "Science, Language and Literacy Case Studies of Learning in Swedish University Physics." PhD diss. University of Uppsala.

Airey, John and Jacob Thøgersen. 2011. "Lecturing undergraduate science in Danish and in English: A comparison of speaking rate and rhetorical style." *English for Specific Purposes* 30:209–221.

Altbach, Philip G. and Jane Knight. 2007. "The internationalization of higher education: motivations and realities." *Journal of Studies in International Education* 11:290–305.

Cameron, Deborah. 2013. "Language, lies and statistics." *Language on the Move*. Accessed June 1 2013. http://www.languageonthemove.com/language-migration-social-justice/language-lies-and-statistics

Cameron, Deborah. 2012a [1995]. *Verbal hygiene.* London: Routledge.

Cameron, Deborah. 2012b. "The one, the many and the Other: representing mono- and multilingualism in post-9/11 verbal hygiene". Paper presented at the conference Multilingualism 2.0, University of Arizona, Tucson, April 13–15. Accessed April 24 2014. https://www.youtube.com/watch?v=wbz5KPQrUAs

Cameron, Deborah. 2000a. *Good to talk?: Living and Working in a Communication Culture.* London: Sage.

Cameron, Deborah. 2000b. "Styling the Worker: Gender and the Commodification of Language in the Globalized Service Economy." *Journal of Sociolinguistics* 4(3): 323–347.

Canagarajah, Suresh. 2007. "After disinvention: Possibilities for communication, community and competence." In *Disinventing and reconstituting languages*, edited by Sinfree Makoni and Alastair Pennycook, 233–239. Clevedon: Multilingual Matters.

Council of Europe. 2011. *Common European Framework of Reference for: Learning, Teaching, Assessment*. Brussels: Council of Europe. Accessed March 12. http://www.coe.int/t/dg4/linguistic/source/framework_en.pdf

Cowie, Claire. 2007. "The accents of outsourcing: the meanings of 'neutral' in the Indian call centre industry." *World Englishes* 26(3):316–330.

Creese, Angela and Adrian Blackledge. 2010. "Translanguaging in the bilingual classroom: A Pedagogy for Learning and teaching?" *The Modern Language Journal* 94:103–115.

Danish Language Council. 2003. *Notat om dansk sprogpolitik* [Proposal on Danish Language Policy]. Copenhagen: Danish Language Council.

Danish Language Council. 2007. *Notat om dansk sprogpolitik* [Proposal on Danish Language Policy]. Copenhagen: Danish Language Council.

Danish Language Council. 2012. *Dansk sprogs status 2012* [The State of the Danish Language]. Copenhagen: Danish Language Council.

Danish Ministry of Culture. 2009. *Sprog til tiden: Regeringens opfølgning på sprogudvalgets rapport*. [Laguage in Time: A follow up from the government]. Copenhagen: Danish Ministry of Culture.

Danish Ministry of Culture. 2008. *Sprog til tiden: Rapport fra Sprogudvalget* [Laguage in Time: A Report from the Language Committee]. Copenhagen: Danish Ministry of Culture.

Danish Ministry of Culture. 2004. *Sprogpolitisk redegørelse* [An Account of Language Policy]. Copenhagen: Danish Ministry of Culture.

Danish Ministry of Culture. 2003. *Sprog på spil. Et udspil til en dansk sprogpolitik* [Language at Stake: A Proposal for a Danish Language Policy]. Copenhagen: Danish Ministry of Culture.

Danish Parliament. 2013. *Spørgsmål om danskundervisning og kontanthjælp* [Question about learning Danish and receiving benefits]. Accessed April 24 2014. http://www.ft.dk/samling/20121/spoergsmaal/S1306/index.htm

Davidsen-Nielsen, David. 2009. *Moders Stemme, Fars Hammer. En debatbog om dansk sprogpolitik* [Mother's Voice, Father's Hammer]. Copenhagen: Union of Teachers of Danish.

Dewey, Martin. 2012. "Towards a post-normative approach: learning the pedagogy of ELF." *Journal of English as a lingua franca* 1(1):141–170.

Dorian, Nancy C. 2004. "Minority and endangered languages." In *The handbook of bilingualism*, edited by Tej K. Bhatia, and William C. Ritchie, 437–459. Oxford: Blackwell.

Duchêne, Alexandre. 2009. "Marketing, Management and Performance: Multilingualism as Commodity in a Tourism Call Centre." *Language Policy* 8:27–50.

Duchêne, Alexandre and Monica Heller. 2008. *Discourses of endangerment: ideology and interest in the defence of languages*. London: Continuum.

EF (Education First). 2011. *English Proficiency Index – Comparing English skills between Countries*. Accessed March 12 2014. http://www.ef.com/epi

European Commission. 2003. *Promoting Language Learning and Linguistic Diversity. An Action Plan 2004–2006.* Brussels: European Commission. Accessed March 12 2014. http://eur-lex.europa.eu/LexUriServ/LexUriServ.do?uri=COM:2003:0449:FIN:en:PDF

Fairclough, Norman. 1993. "Critical Discourse Analysis and the Marketization of Public Discourse: The Universities." *Discourse & Society* 4(2): 133–168.

García, Ofelia. 2009. *Bilingual education in the 21st century: A global perspective.* Oxford: Wiley.

Gazzola, Michele. 2012. "The linguistic implications of academic performance indicators: general trends and case study." *International Journal of the Sociology of Language* 216:131–156.

Gazzola, Michele and Francois Grin. 2013. "Is ELF more effective and fair than translation? An evaluation of the EU's multilingual regime." *International Journal of Applied Linguistics* 23(1):93–107.

Haberland, Hartmut, Dorte Lønsmann and Bent Preisler. 2013. *Language Alternation, Language Choice and Language Encounter in International Tertiary Education.* Dordrecht: Springer.

Haberland, Hartmut, Carol Henriksen, Robert Phillipson and Tove Skutnabb-Kangas. 1991. "Tak for mad! Om sprogæderi med dansk som livret" [Thanks for the meal: On language cannibalism]. In *Det danske sprogs status år 2001: Er dansk et truet sprog?* [The State of the Danish Language 2001: Is Danish a Threatened Language?], edited by Jens Normann Jørgensen, 111–138. Copenhagen: The Pedagogical University of Denmark.

Harder, Peter. 2009. *English in Denmark – Language Policy, Internationalization and University Teaching.* Copenhagen: Museum Tusculanum Press.

Hazelkorn, Ellen. 2011. *Rankings and the Reshaping of Higher Education: The Battle for World-Class Excellence.* Basingstoke: Palgrave Macmillan.

Hellekjær, Glenn Ole. 2010. "Lecture Comprehension in English-Medium Higher Education." *Hermes - Journal of Language and Communication Studies* 45:11–34.

Hellekjær, Glenn Ole. 2007. "The implementation of undergraduate level English medium programs in Norway: An explorative case study." In *Researching content and language integration in higher education*, edited by Robert Wilkin and Vera Zegars, 68–81. Maastricht: Universitaire Pers Maastricht.

Heller, Monica. 2003. "Globalization the new economy, and the commodification of language and identity." *Journal of Sociolinguistics* 7(4):473–492.

Hultgren, Anna Kristina. 2011. "'Building rapport' with customers across the world: the global diffusion of a call centre speech style." *Journal of Sociolinguistics* 15(1):36–64.

Hultgren, Anna Kristina. 2013. *Parallelsproglighed på danske universiteter: En statusrapport 2013* [Parallellingualism at Danish universities: A status report 2013]. Copenhagen: Centre for Internationalisation and Parallel Language Use. Accessed March 12 2014. http://nordiskparallelsprogsnet.blogs.ku.dk/files/2013/04/LanderapportDK_V4.pdf

Hultgren, Anna Kristina. 2014. "Whose Parallellingualism? Overt and Covert Ideologies in Danish University Language Policies. *Multilingua*". *Journal of Cross-Cultural and Interlanguage Communication* 33(1-2):61–87.

Jakobsen, Anne Sofie. 2010. *'Ellers er det lige ud af landevejen' - En interviewundersøgelse af ti underviseres holdninger til og erfaringer med engelsksproget undervisning ved Det Biovidenskabelige Fakultet, KU*

['You just get on with it' – An interview study of ten teachers attitudes to and experiences with English-language instruction at The Bio Science Faculty, University of Copenhagen]. Copenhagen: University of Copenhagen Faculty of Humanities.

Jarvad, Pia. 2001. *Det danske sprogs status i 1990'erne med særligt henblik på domænetab* [The State of the Danish Language in the 1990s with special regard to domain loss]. Copenhagen: Danish Language Council.

Jarvad, Pia. 2008. *De nordiske sprog og engelsk ved nordiske universiteter, højskoler og andre højere læreanstalter* [The Nordic languages and English at Nordic Universities and other further and higher education institutions]. København: Copenhagen: Danish Language Council.

Jaspers, Jürgen. 2011. "Talking like a 'zerolingual': Ambiguous linguistic caricatures at an urban secondary school." *Journal of Pragmatics* 43:1264–1278.

Jenkins, Jennifer, Alessia Cogo and Martin Dewey. 2011. "Review of developments in research into English as a Lingua Franca." *Language Teaching* 44(3):281–315.

Jensen, Christian, Louise Denver Inger M. Mees & Charlotte Werther. 2013. "Students' attitudes to lecturers' English in English-medium higher education in Denmark." *Nordic Journal of English Studies* 12(1):87–112.

Jensen, Christian & Jacob Thøgersen. 2011. "Danish University lecturers' attitudes towards English as the medium of instruction." *Ibérica* 22:13–34.

Jørgensen, Jens Norman. 2008. "Polylingual languaging around and among children and adolescents." *International Journal of Multilingualism* 5(3):161–176.

Jørgensen, Jens Norman and Anne Holmen. 2010. *Sprogs status i Danmark 2021* [The state of languages in Denmark]. Copenhagen: The Copenhagen Studies in Bilingualism.

Kirchmeier-Andersen, Sabine. 2008. "Lov til dansk?" [A language policy for Danish?] *Jyllands-Posten.* 7 April.

Klaassen, Renate. 2001. "The international university curriculum: Challenges in English-medium engineering education." PhD diss. University of Technology Delft.

Klaassen, Renate and Madeleine Bos. 2010. "English Language Screening for Scientific Staff at Delft University of Technology." *Hermes – Journal of Language and Communication Studies* 45:61–75.

Makihara, Miki and Bambi B. Shieffelin. 2007. *Consequences of contact: language ideologies and sociocultural transformations in Pacific societies.* Oxford: Oxford University Press.

Møller, Janus Spindler. 2008. "Polylingual performance among Turkish-Danes in late-modern Copenhagen." *International Journal of Multilingualism* 5(3):217–236.

Nordic Council of Ministers. 2007. *Declaration on Nordic Language Policy.* Copenhagen: Nordic Council of Ministers.

Otsuji, Emi and Alastair Pennycook. 2010. "Metrolingualism: fixity, fluidity and language in

Flux." *Journal of Multilingualism* 7(3):240–254.

Phillipson, Robert. 2015. "English as threat or opportunity in European higher education" In *English-Medium Instruction in European Higher Education* edited by Slobodanka Dimova, Anna Kristina Hultgren, and Christian Jensen. Berlin: Mouton.

Phillipson, Robert. 2006. "English, a cuckoo in the European higher education nest of languages?" *European Journal of English Studies* 10(1):13–32.

Preisler, Bent. 1999. *Danskerne og det engelske sprog* [The Danes and the English Language]. Roskile: Roskilde Universitetsforlag.

Saarinen, Taina and Tarja Nikula. 2013. Implicit policy, invisible language: policies and practices of international degree programmes in higher education. In *English-medium instruction at universities: global challenges* edited by Aintzane Doiz, David Lasagabaster, and Juan Manuel Sierra, 131–150. Bristol: Multilingual Matters.

Seidlhofer, Barbara. 2011. *Understanding English as a Lingua Franca*. Oxford: Oxford University Press.

Siiner, Maarja. 2010. "Hangovers of globalization: a case study of laissez-faire language policy in Denmark." *Language Problems & Language Planning* 34(1):43–62.

Taylor, Lynda. 2006. "The Changing Landscape of English: implications for language Assessment." *ELT Journal* 60(1):51–59.

Taylor, Phil, Jeff Hyman, Gareth Mulvey, and Peter Bain. 2002. "Work Organization, Control, and the Experience of Work in Call Centres." *Work, Employment and Society* 16(1):133–150.

Vinke, Adriana Anthonia. 1995. "English as the medium of instruction in Dutch engineeering education." PhD diss. University of Technology Delft.

Airey, John. 2009. "Science, Language and Literacy Case Studies of Learning in Swedish University Physics." PhD diss. University of Uppsala.

Contributors

Rita Cancino,
Associate professor in Spanish, Aalborg University, Denmark

Lotte Dam
Associate professor in Spanish, Aalborg University, Denmark

Jesper Bonderup Frederiksen
PhD student in English, Aalborg University, Denmark

Anna Kristina Hultgren
Lecturer in English, The Open University, UK

Kim Ebensgaard Jensen
Associate professor in English, Aalborg University, Denmark

Aase Voldgaard Larsen
Associate professor in German, Aalborg University, Denmark

Richard Madsen
PhD student in English, Aalborg University, Denmark